The Chic Cartoon Book

By
Arnold Wiles

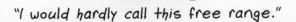

"I would hardly call this free range."

ISBN 978-1-904871-99-6

A catalogue record for this book is available from
the British Library.

Published by

The Good Life Press Ltd.,

The Old Pigsties, Clifton Fields,

Lytham Road, Preston, PR4 0XG

www.goodlifepress.co.uk

www.homefarmer.co.uk

Since his first published cartoon in Punch magazine in the 1940s, Arnold Wiles has been entertaining generations of country lovers with his witty and clever cartoons. He even featured in one of Jack Hargreaves' Out of Town programmes in the 1960s due to Jack's love of his fishing cartoons. Indeed, Jack Hargreaves went on to say that Arnold Wiles "is the finest angling cartoonist that this country has ever produced."

He has published several cartoon books including Motorist at Large, Away from it All, Wiles on the Water and a Pretty Kettle of Fish, as well as being a stock cartoonist for Punch magazine and numerous rural titles.

This book, specially commissioned by The Good Life Press, features 60 new cartoons for a new audience. Arnold has lost none of his sharpness and wit and brings together captions and cartoons that will make the reader chuckle, chicken keeper or not.

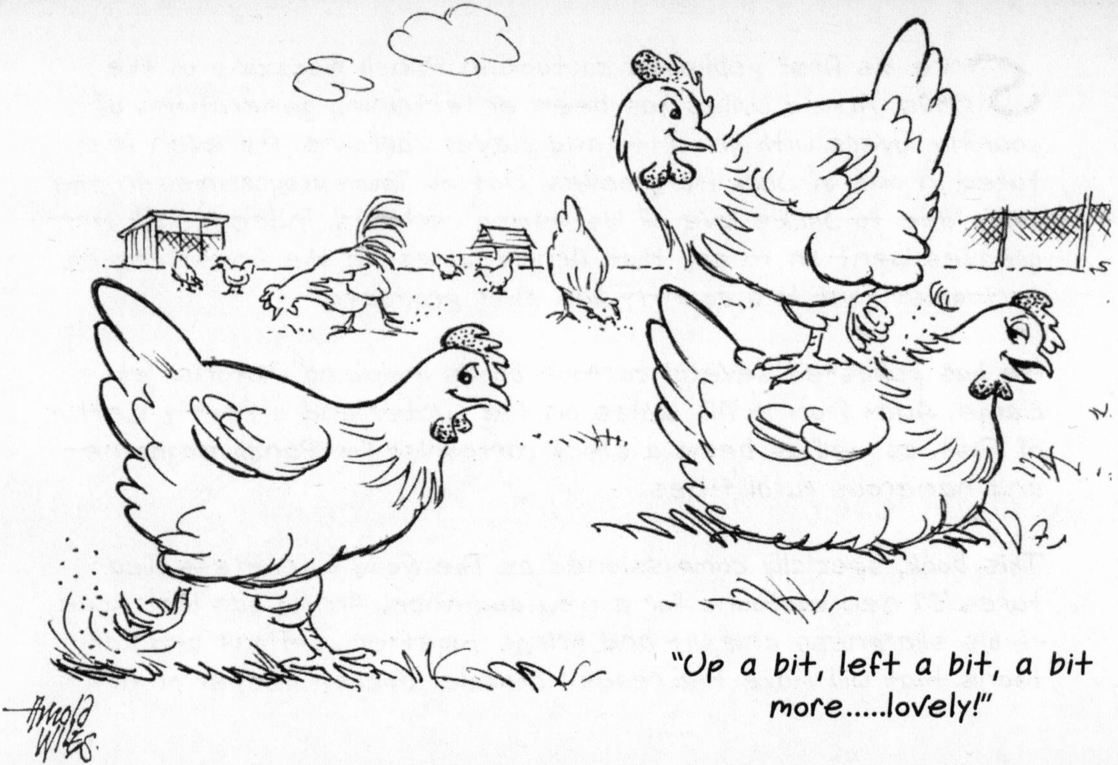
Arnold Wiles

"Up a bit, left a bit, a bit more.....lovely!"

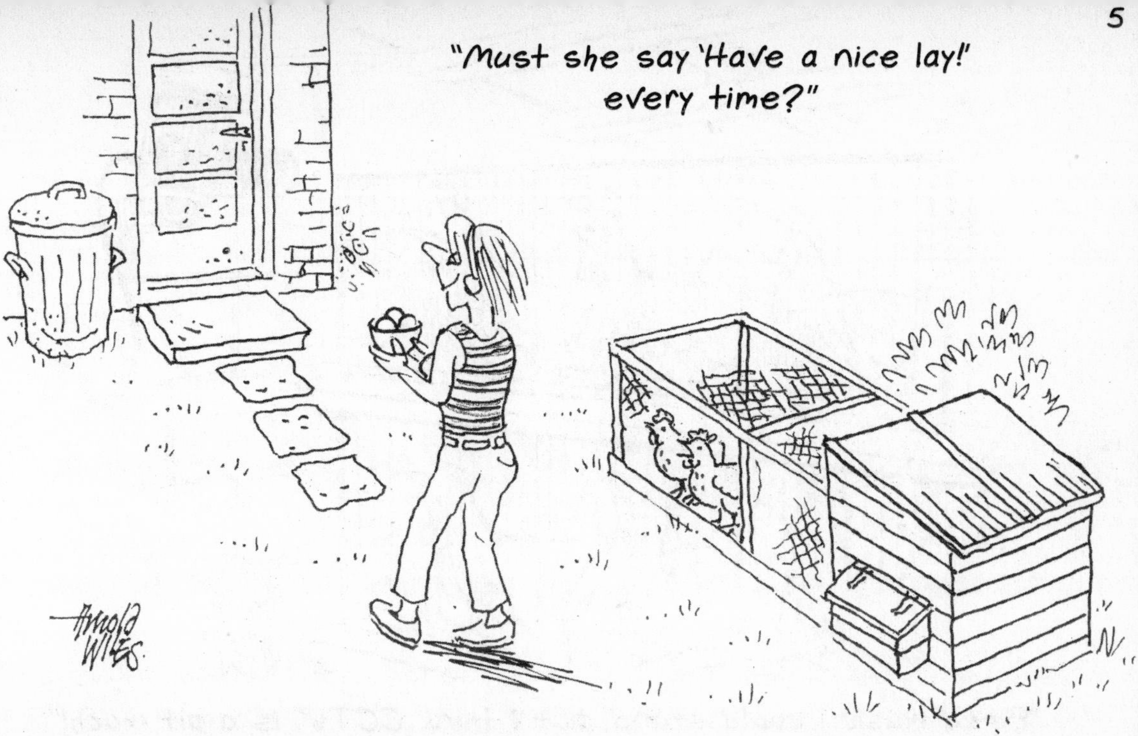
Arnold Wiles

"Must she say 'Have a nice lay!' every time?"

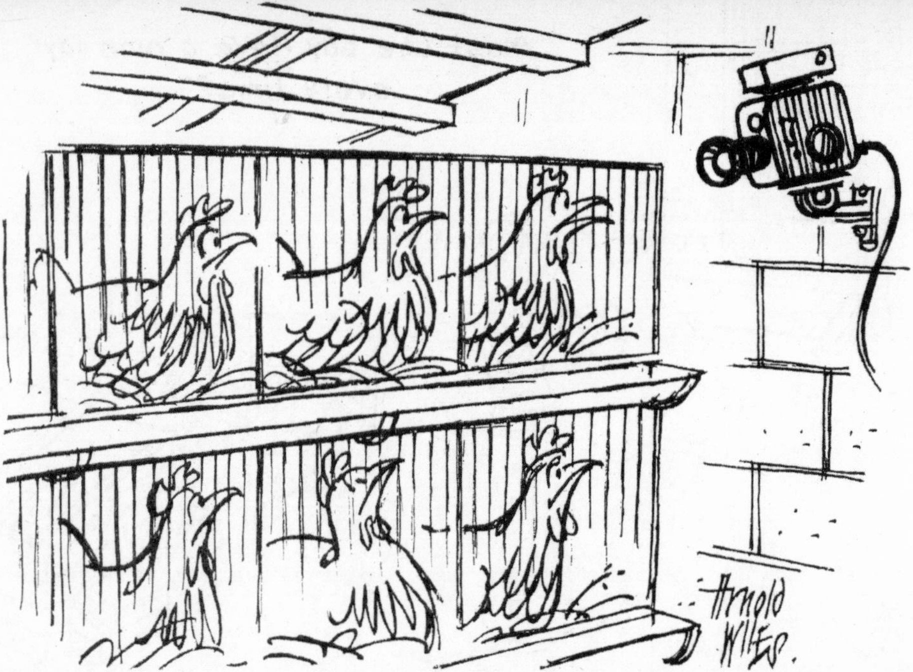
Arnold Wiles

"Piped music I could stand, but I think CCTV is a bit much!"

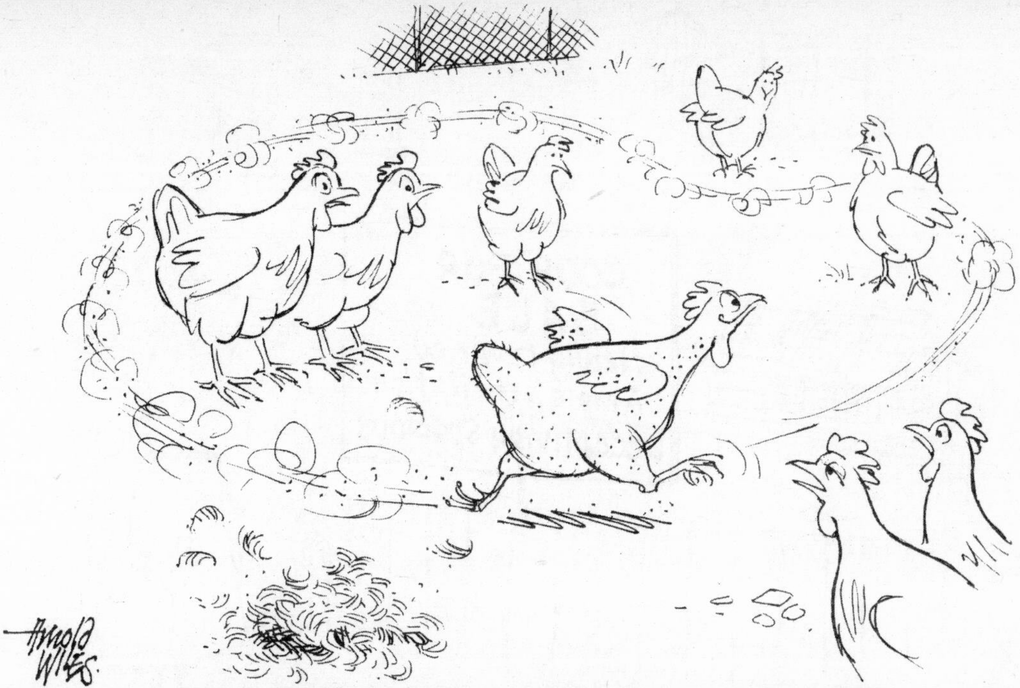

"I suppose we just had to have a streaker sooner or later."

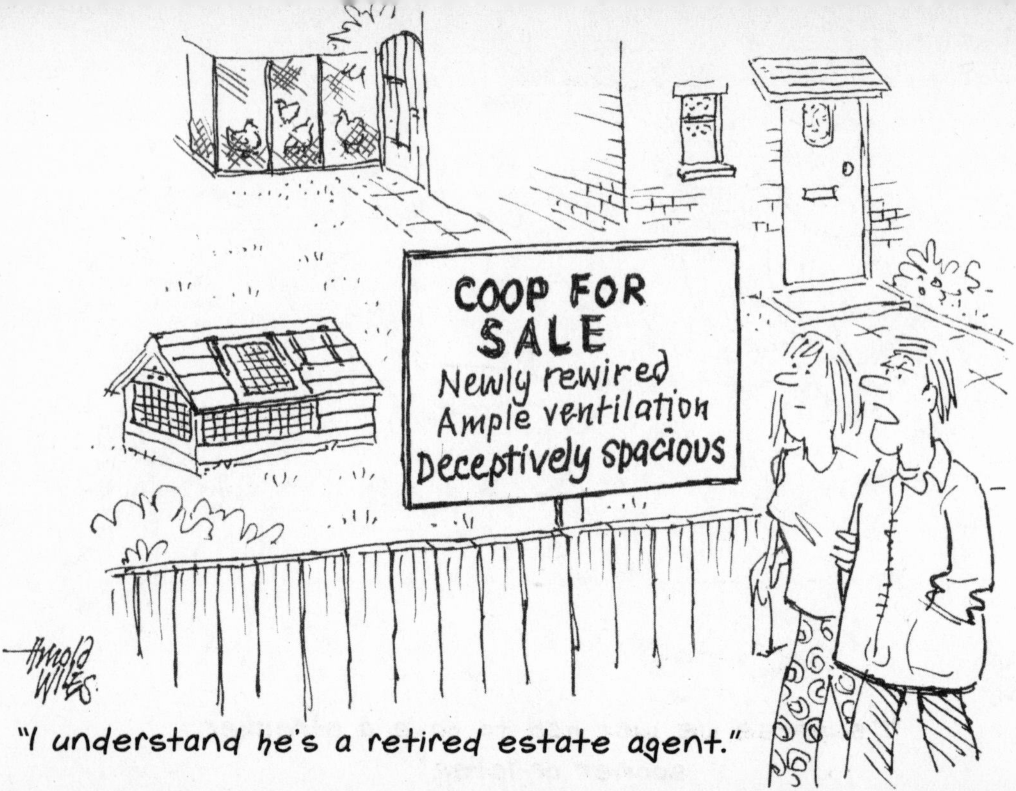
COOP FOR SALE
Newly rewired
Ample ventilation
Deceptively spacious
Arnold Wiles

"I understand he's a retired estate agent."

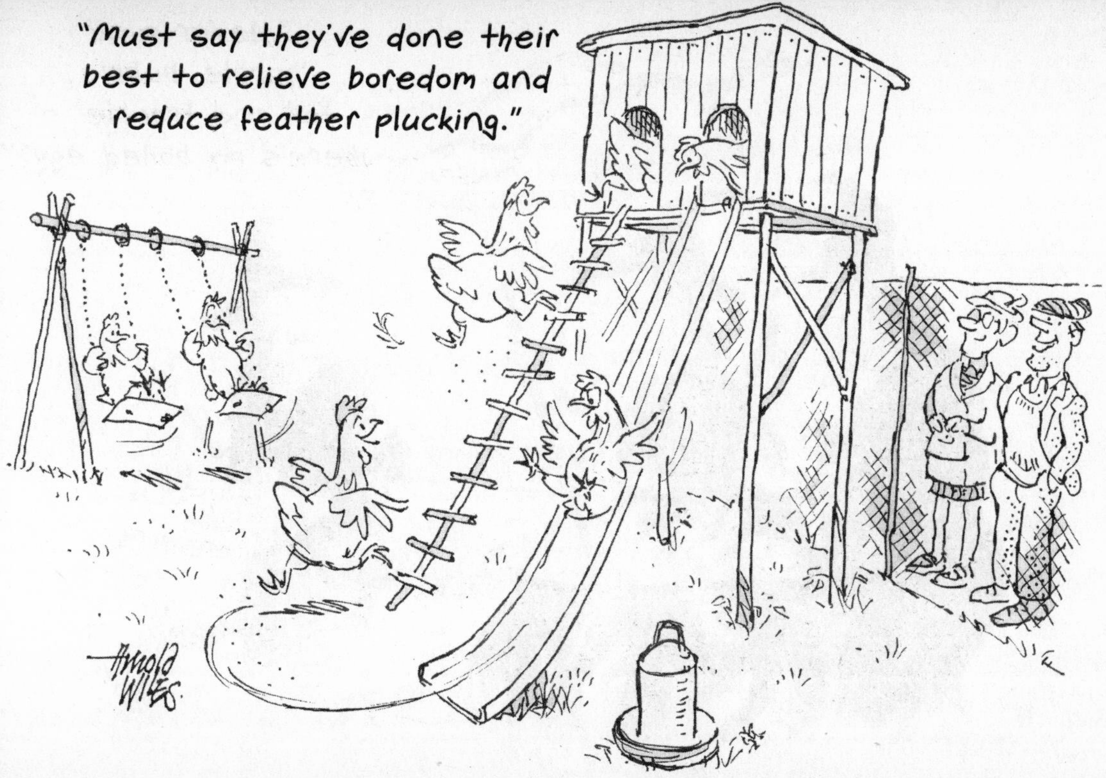

"Must say they've done their best to relieve boredom and reduce feather plucking."

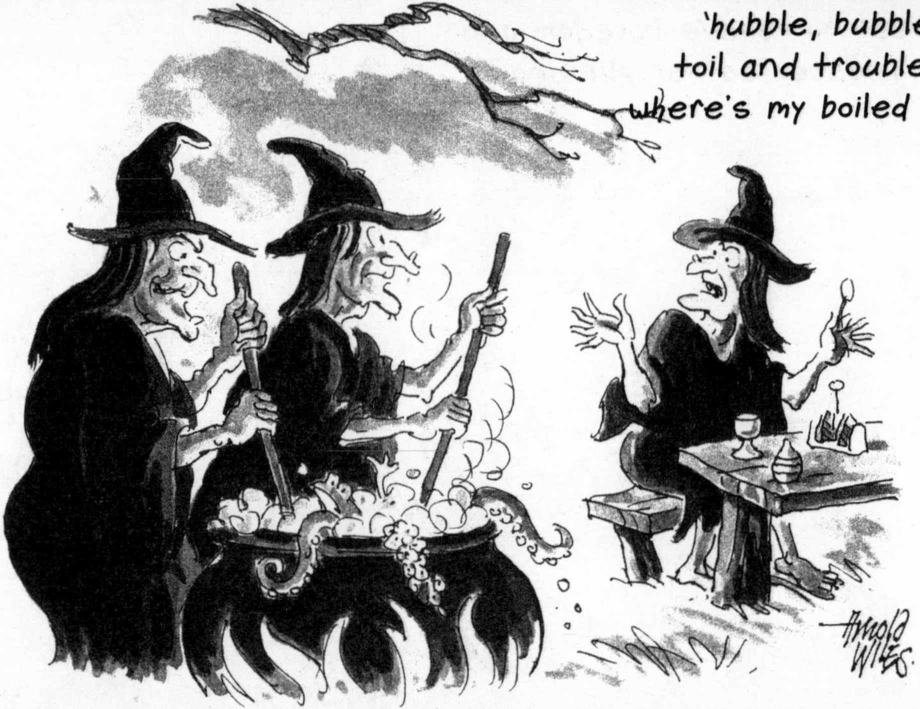
Arnold Wiles

"Never mind 'hubble, bubble, toil and trouble' – where's my boiled egg?"

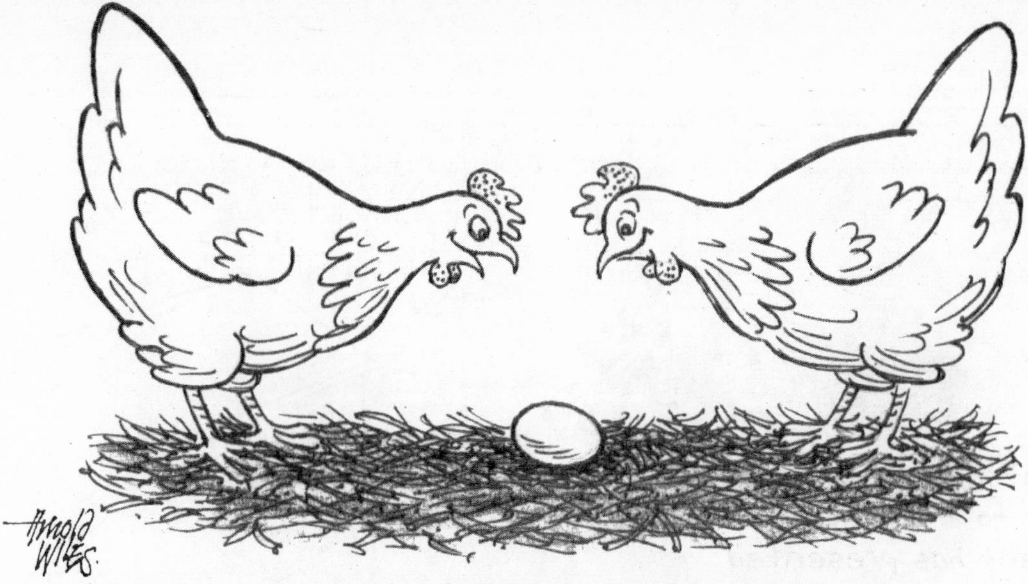
Arnold Wiles

"Cute at that age, aren't they?"

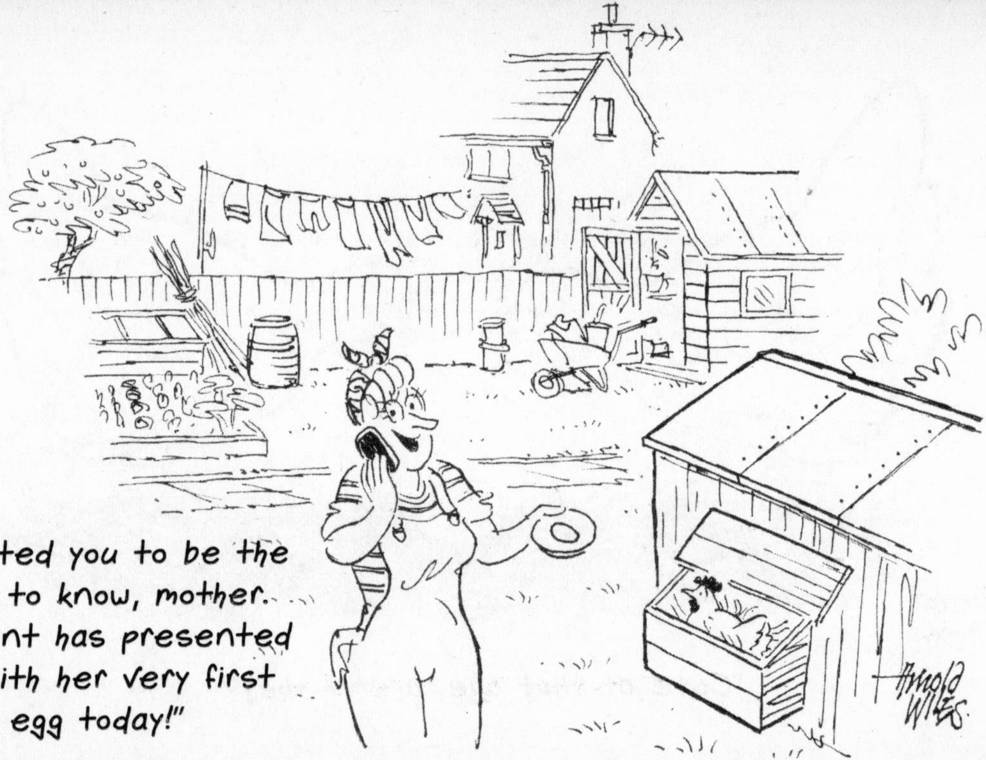
Arnold Wiles

"I wanted you to be the first to know, mother. Millicent has presented me with her very first egg today!"

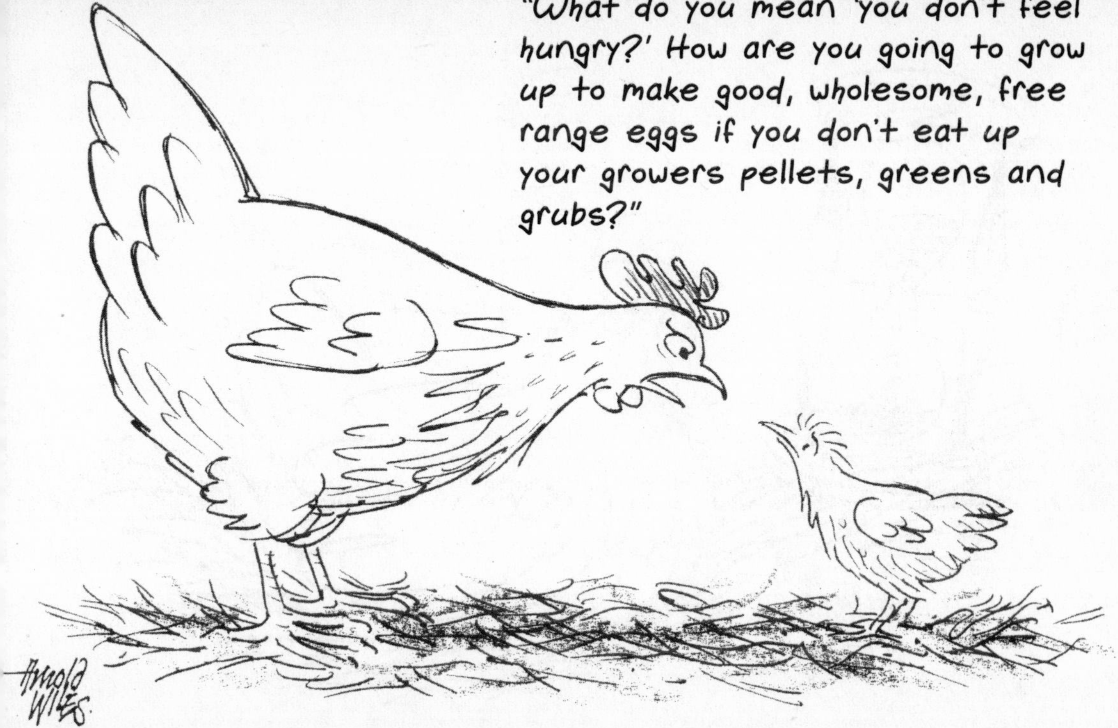

"What do you mean 'you don't feel hungry?' How are you going to grow up to make good, wholesome, free range eggs if you don't eat up your growers pellets, greens and grubs?"

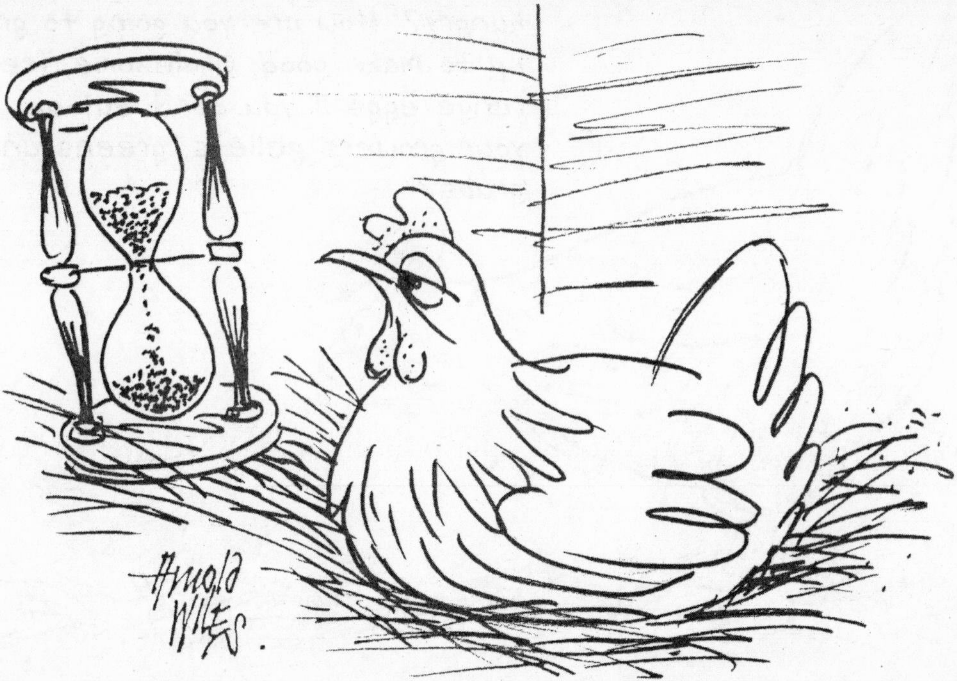

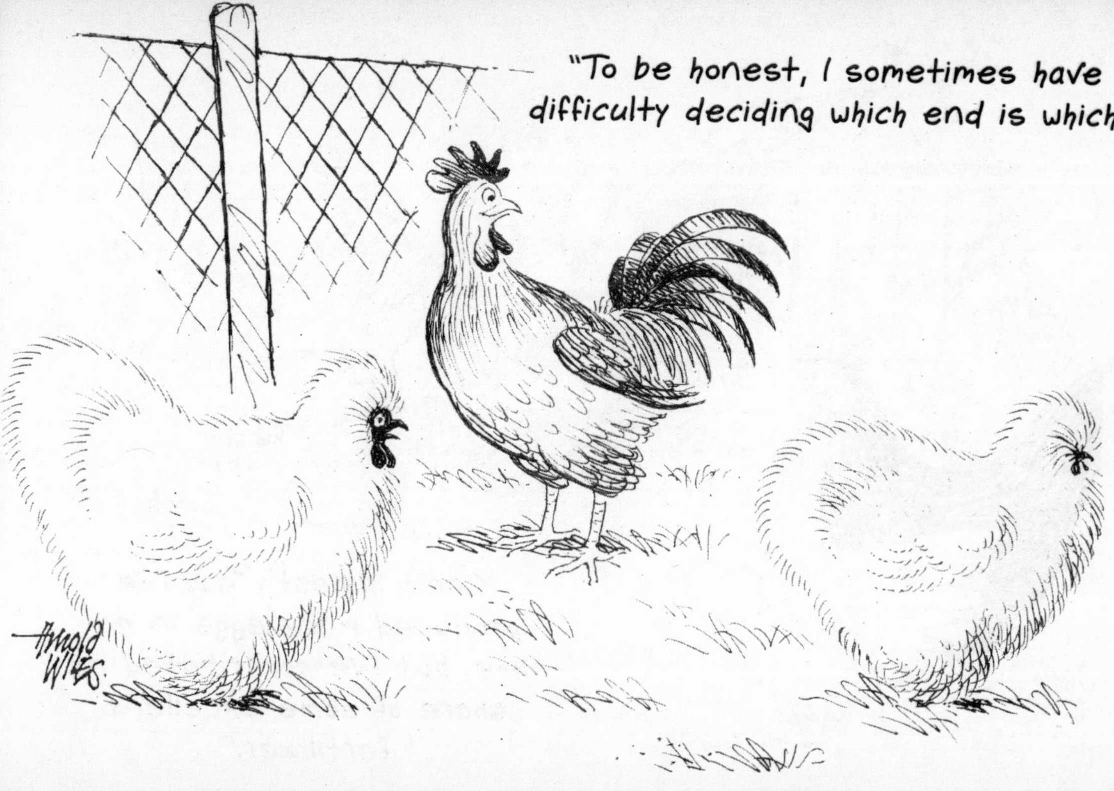
Arnold Wiles

"To be honest, I sometimes have difficulty deciding which end is which."

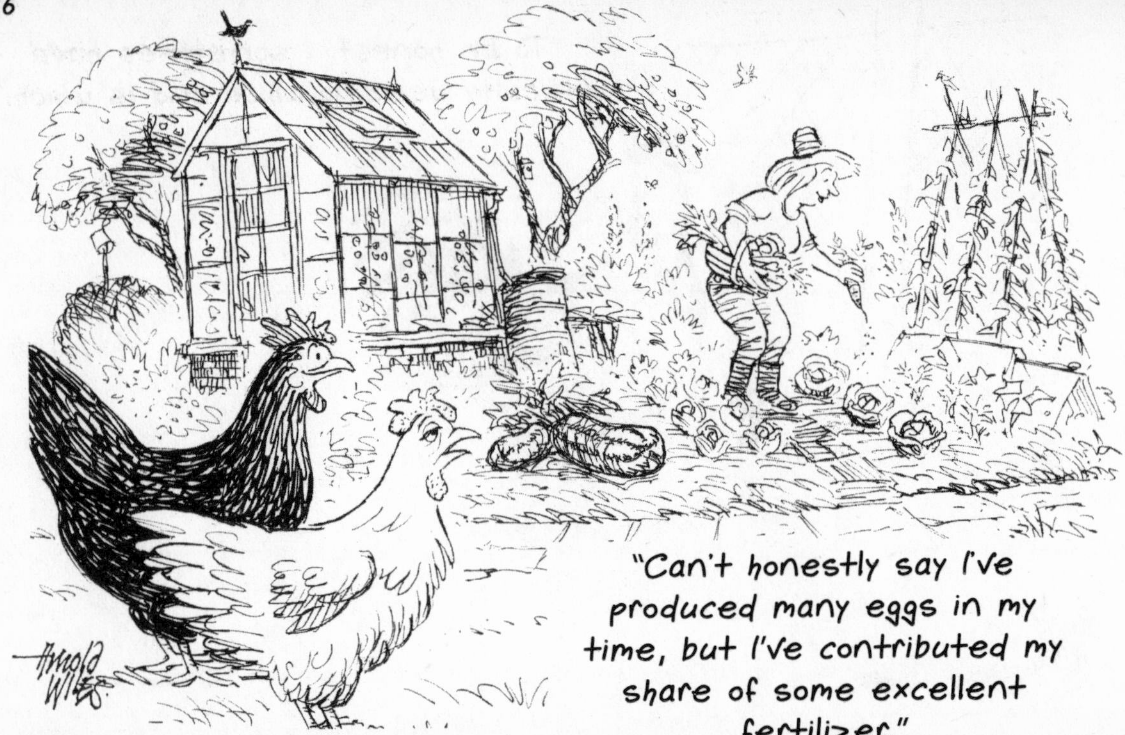
Arnold Wiles

"Can't honestly say I've produced many eggs in my time, but I've contributed my share of some excellent fertilizer."

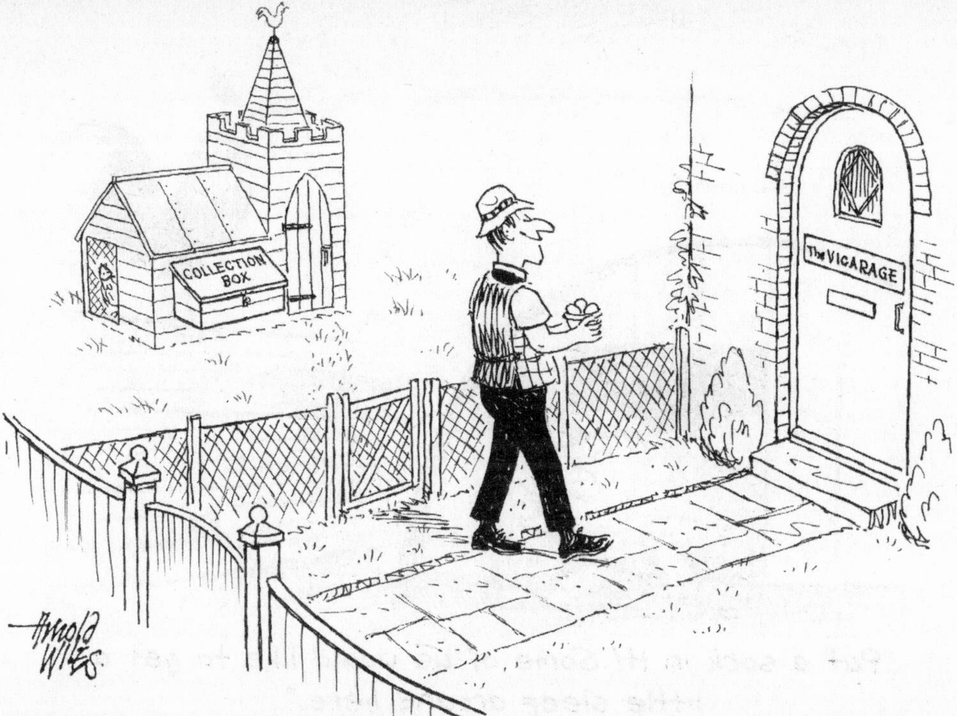
COLLECTION BOX
The VICARAGE

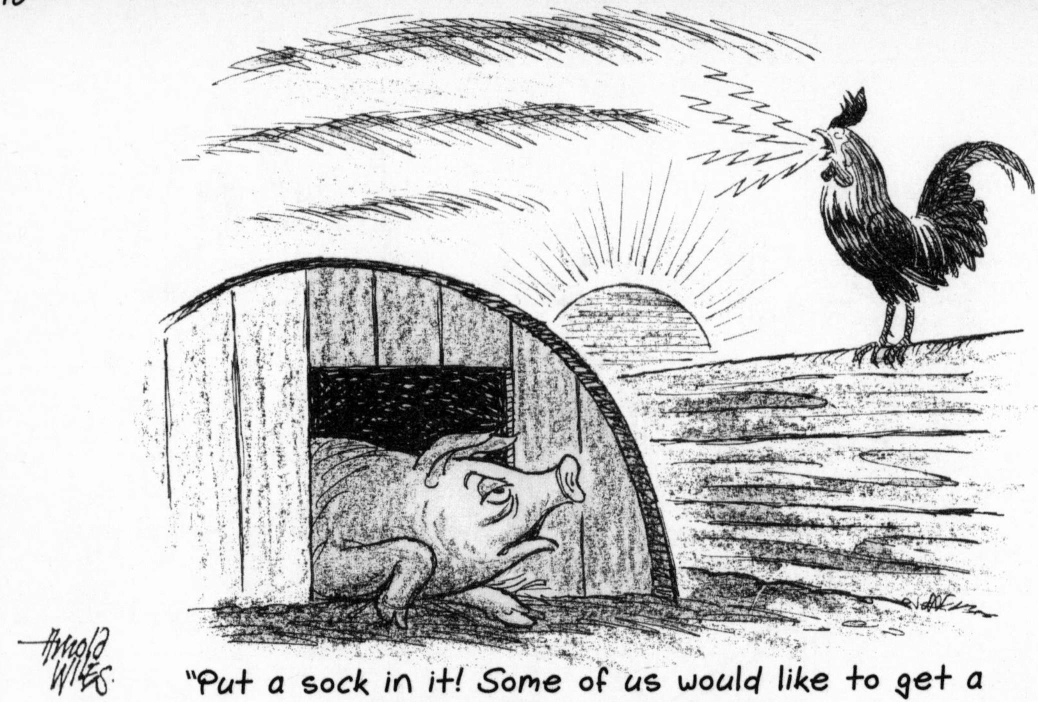

"Put a sock in it! Some of us would like to get a little sleep around here."

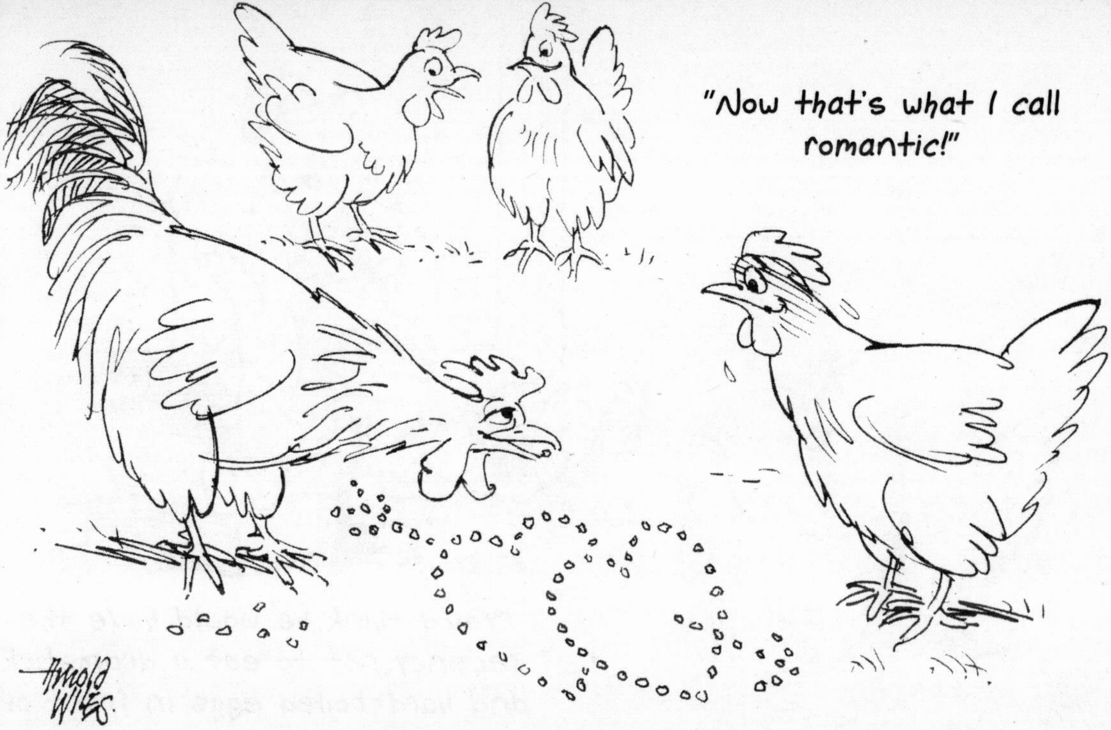
Arnold Wiles

"Now that's what I call romantic!"

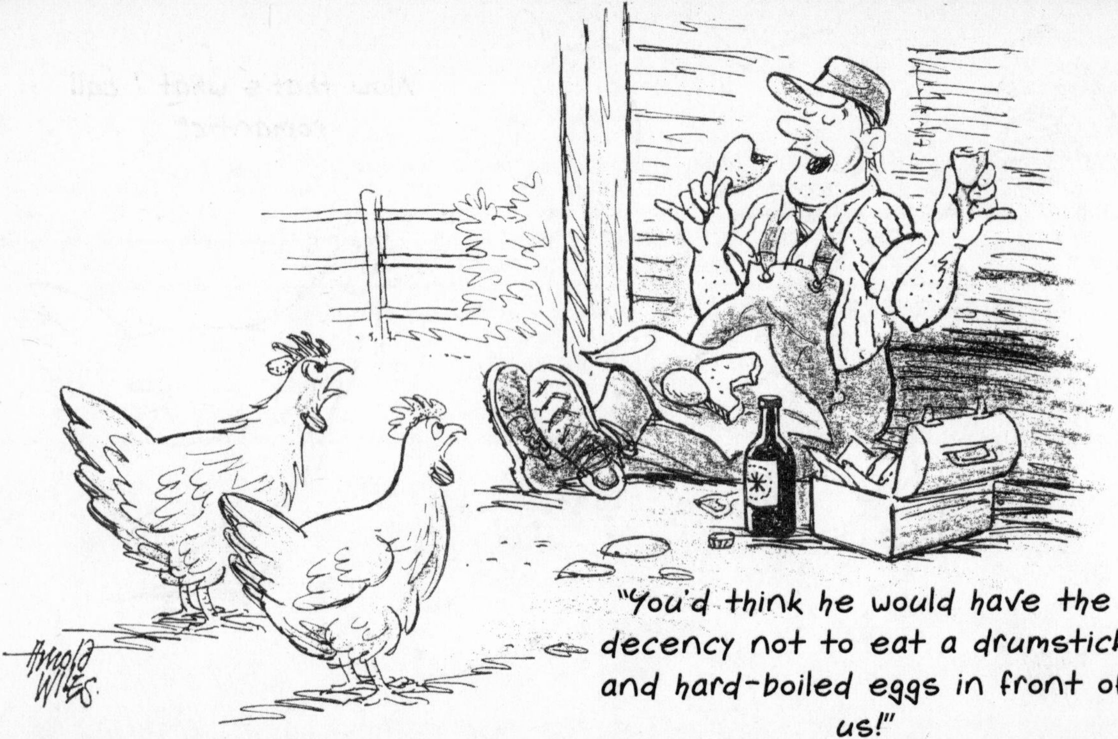
Arnold Wiles

"You'd think he would have the decency not to eat a drumstick and hard-boiled eggs in front of us!"

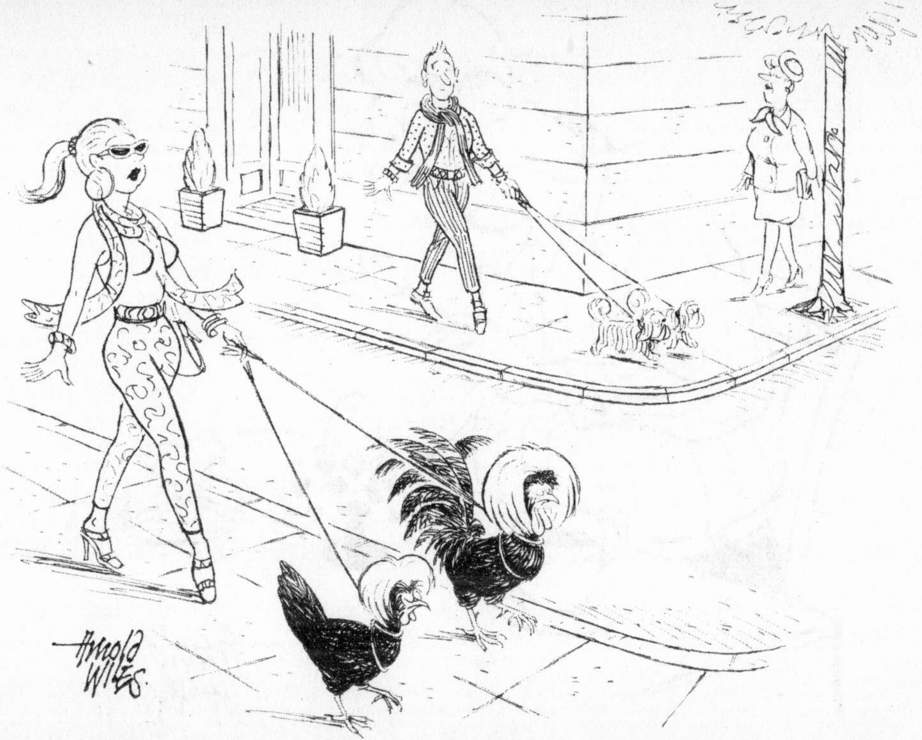
Arnold Wiles

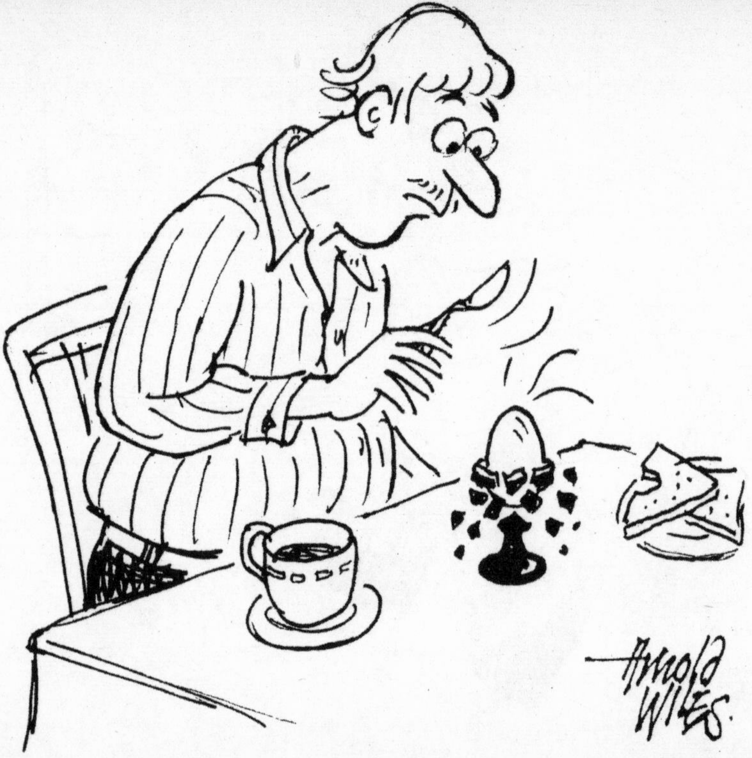
Arnold
WILES.

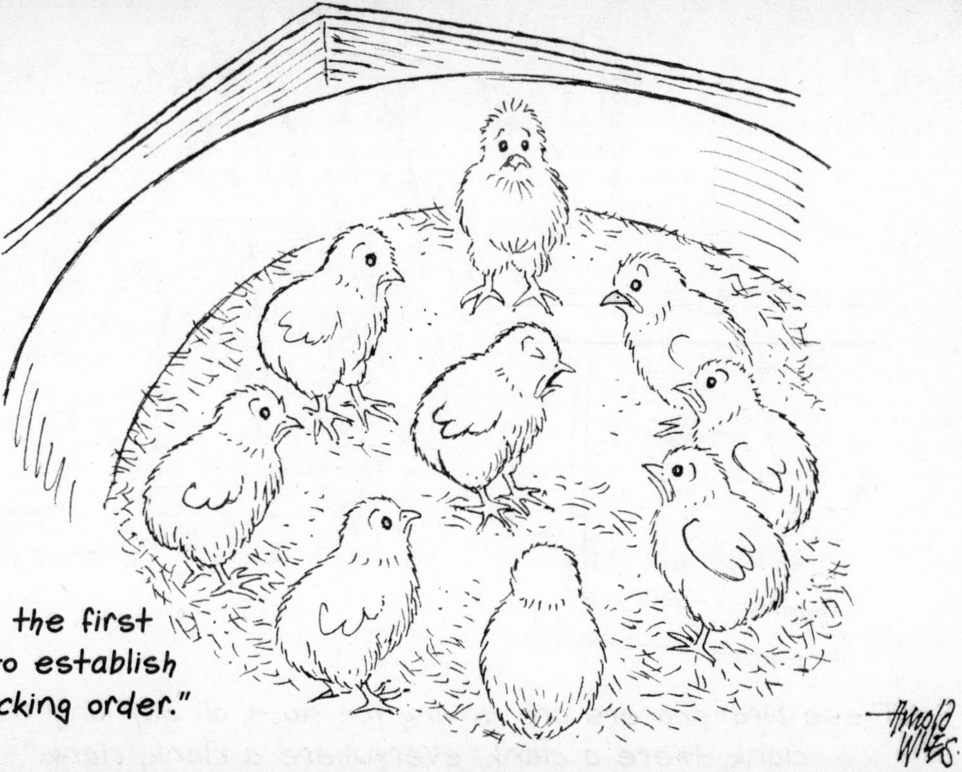
Arnold Wiles

"Now the first thing to establish is a pecking order."

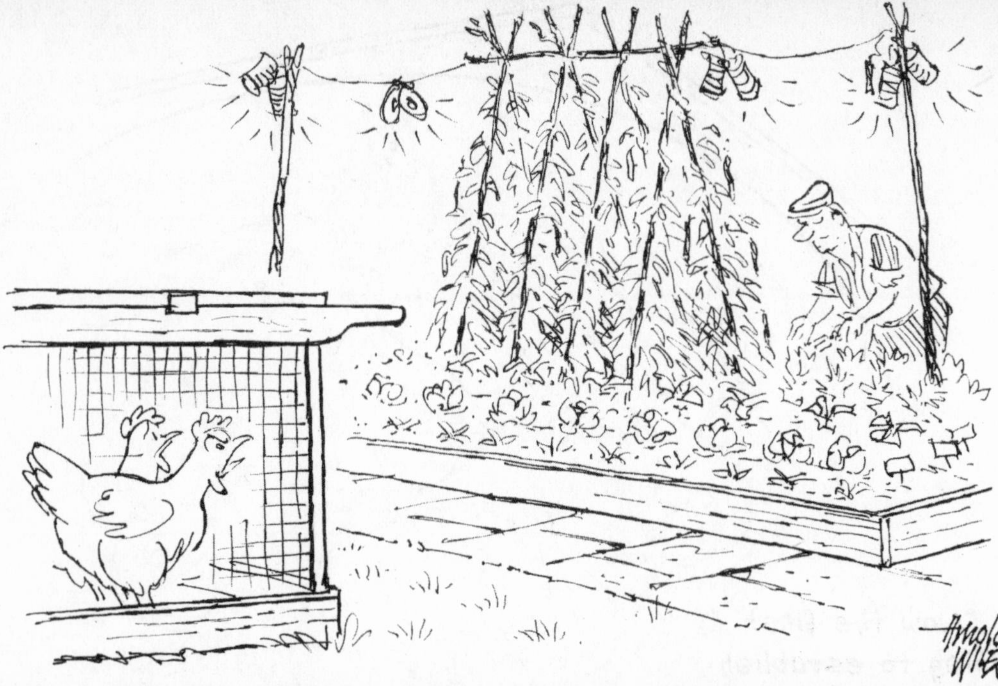
Arnold Wiles

"These bird-scarers are driving me nuts all day long! Here a clank, there a clank, everywhere a clank, clank."

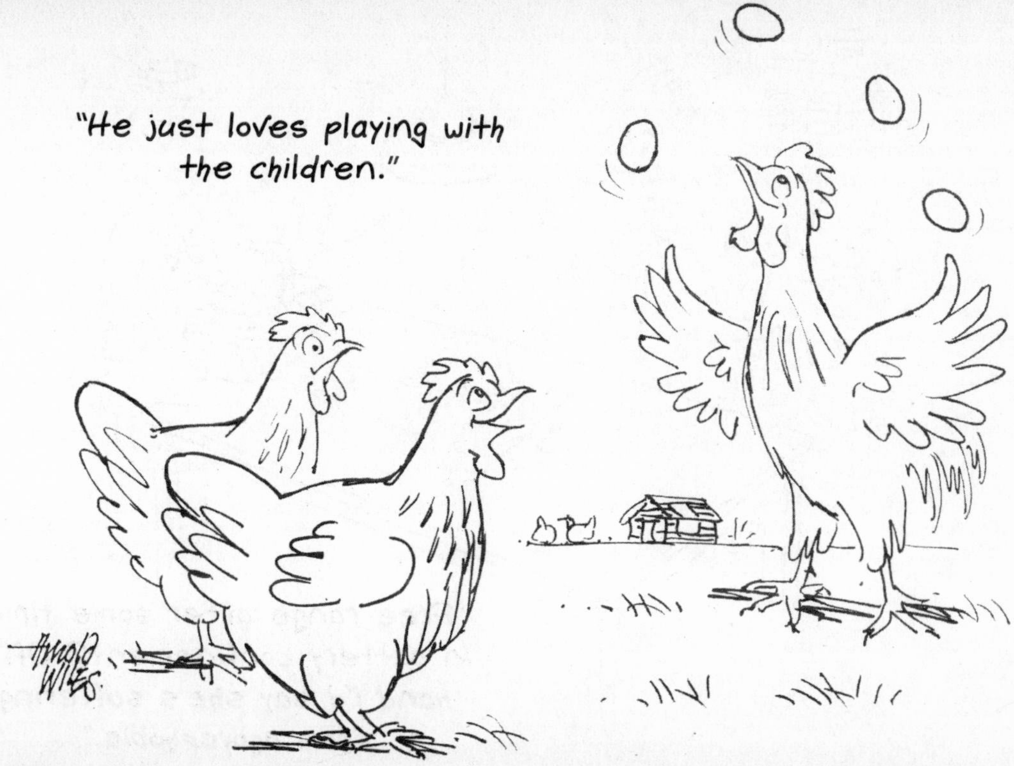
Arnold Wiles

"He just loves playing with the children."

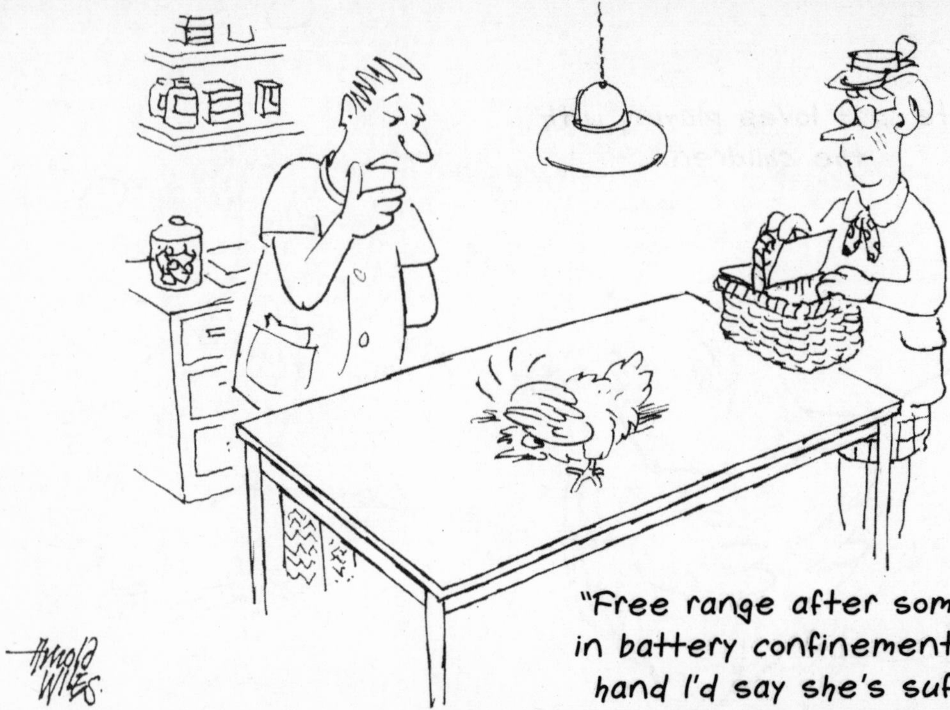
Arnold Wiles

"Free range after some time in battery confinement? Off-hand I'd say she's suffering from agoraphobia."

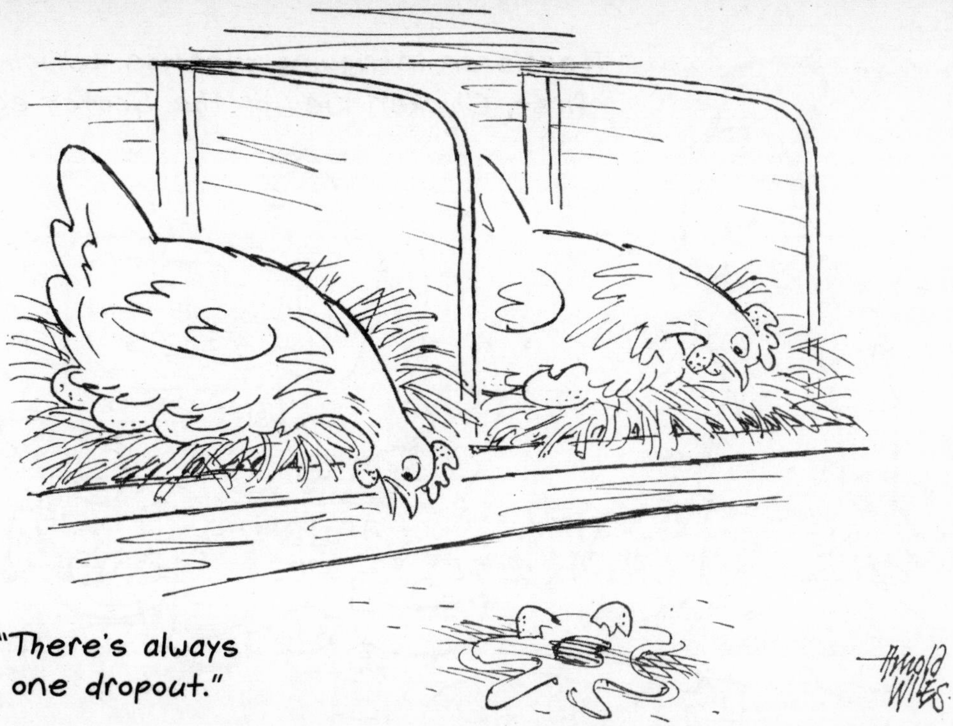

"There's always one dropout."

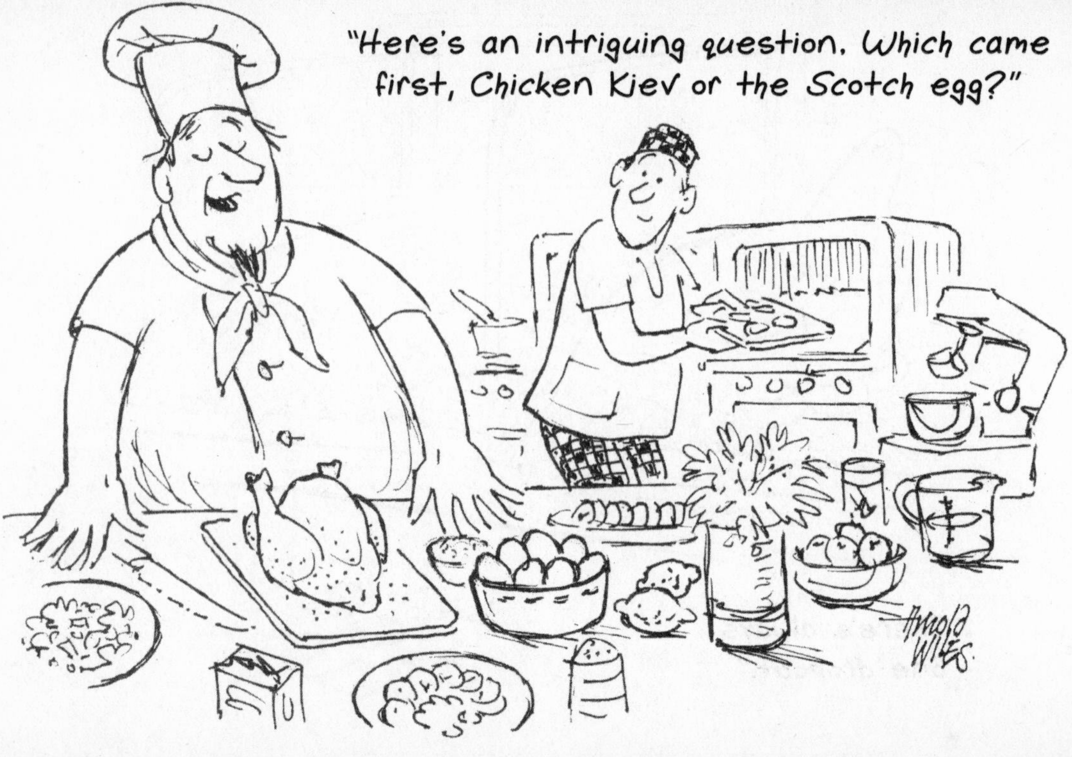

"Here's an intriguing question. Which came first, Chicken Kiev or the Scotch egg?"

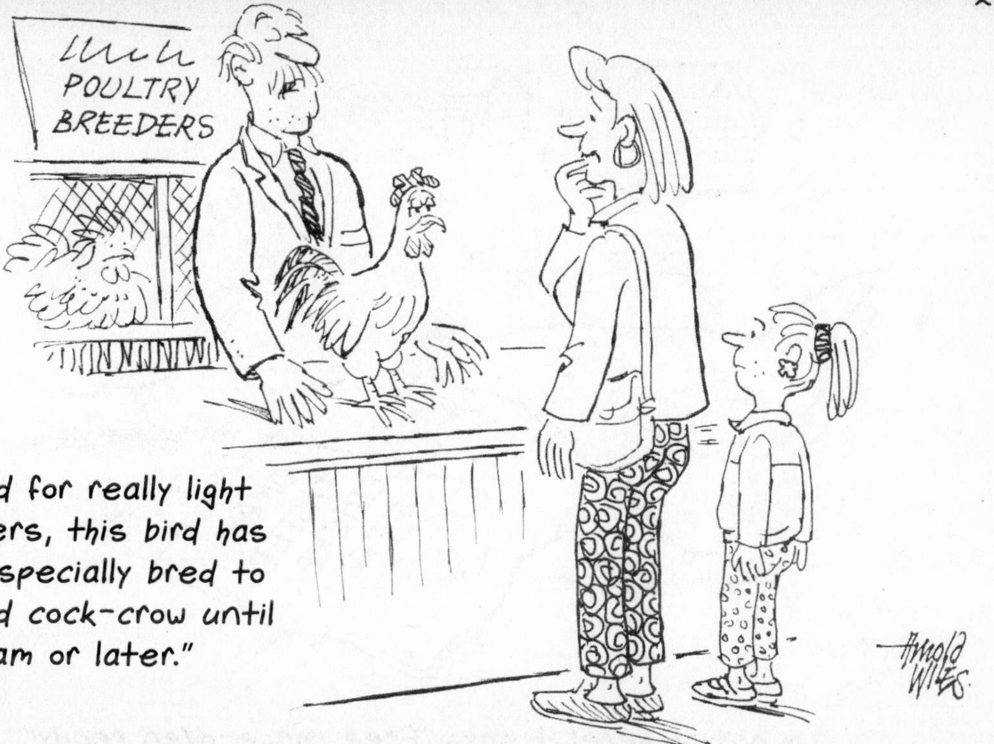
POULTRY
BREEDERS
Arnold WILES

"...and for really light sleepers, this bird has been specially bred to withhold cock-crow until 7am or later."

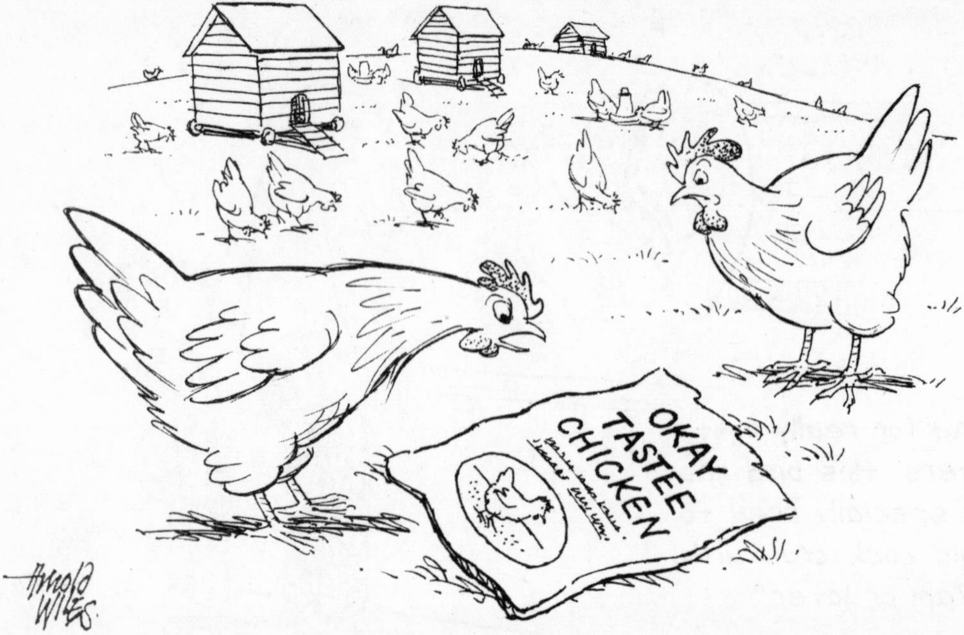
OKAY
TASTEE
CHICKEN

"I'm out of here! It says 'Free range-oven ready!'"

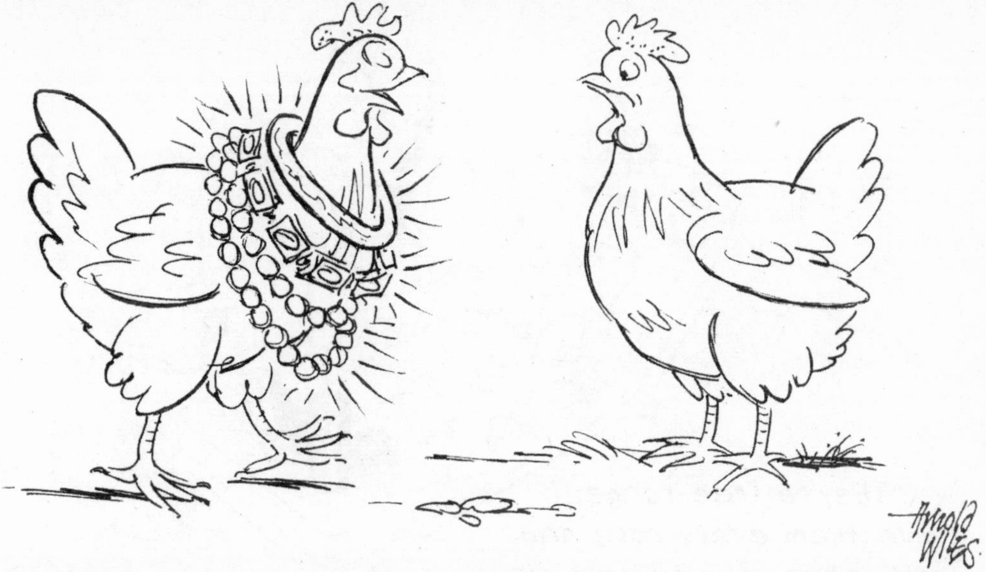
Arnold Wiles

"Oh these? I was just scratching around when I happened to uncover a rusty old box."

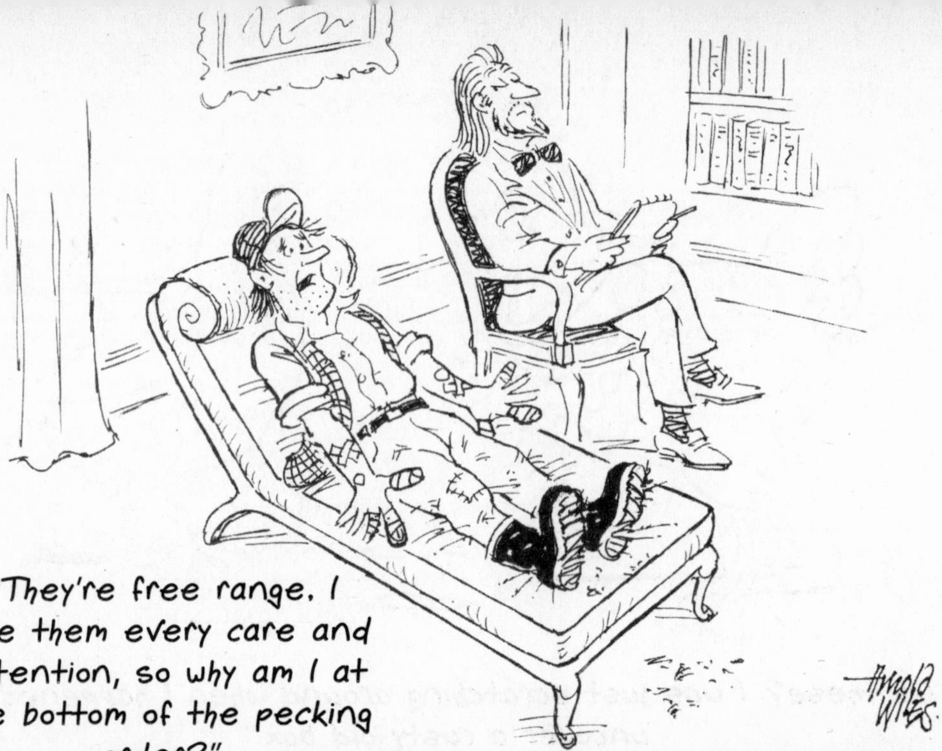
Arnold
WILES

"They're free range. I give them every care and attention, so why am I at the bottom of the pecking order?"

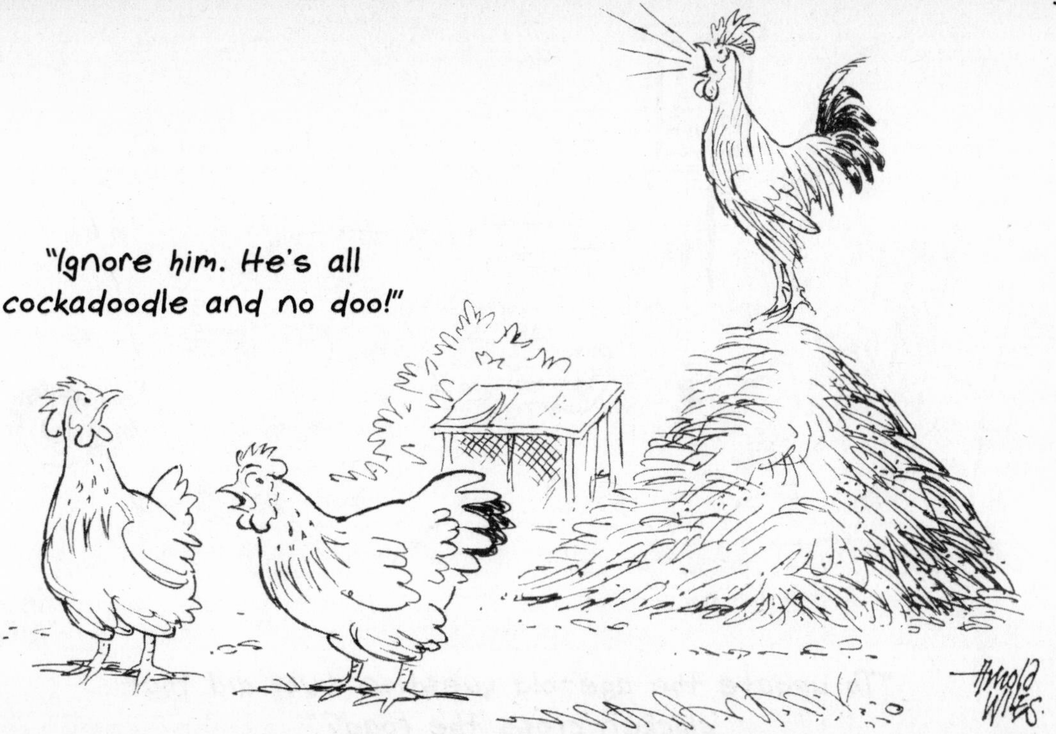
Arnold Wiles

"Ignore him. He's all cockadoodle and no doo!"

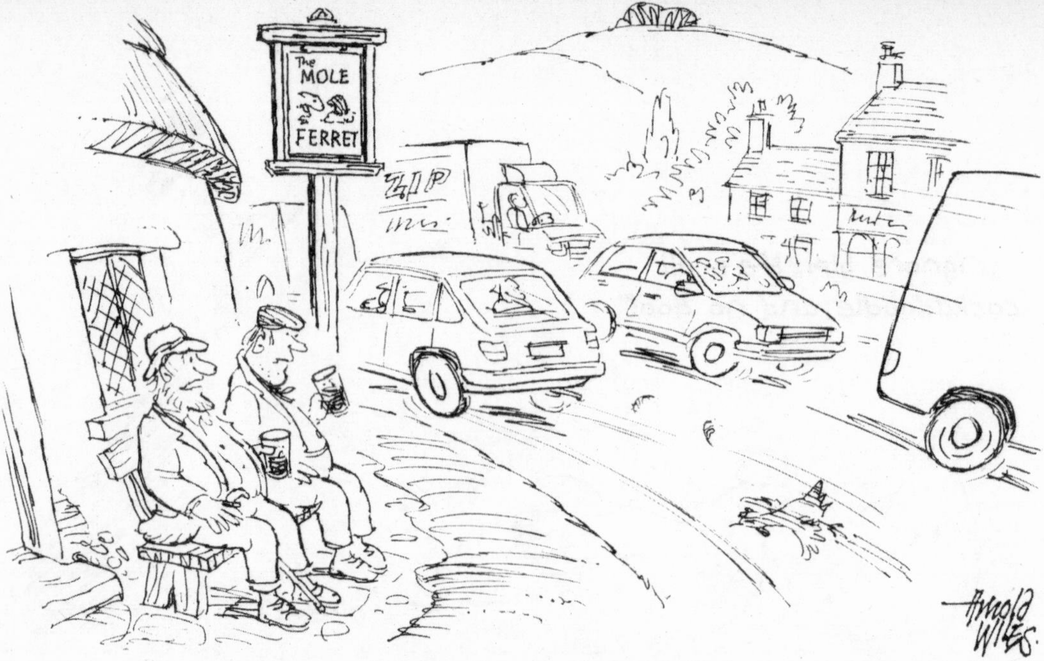
The MOLE
FERRET
ZIP

"To update the age-old question: Why did that chicken cross the road?"

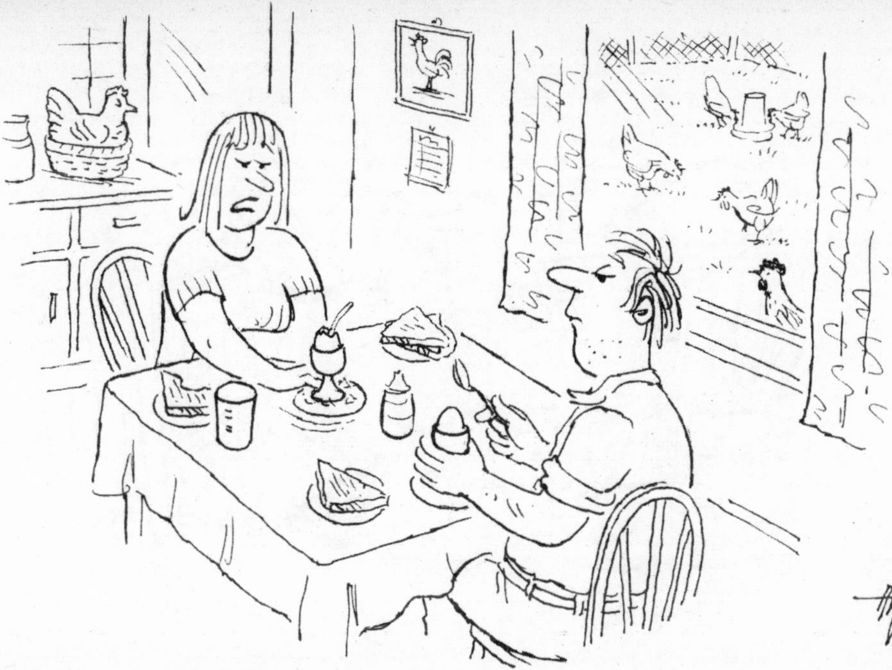

"Soft-boiled, hard-boiled, poached, scrambled or fried - I couldn't face another egg for at least a fortnight."

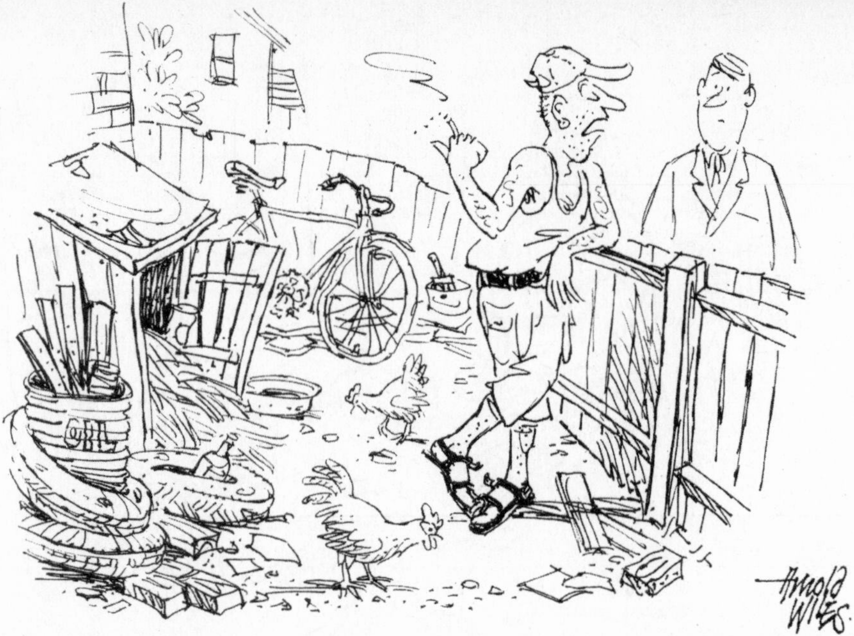

"I always say you can't beat keeping 'em free range in their natural environment."

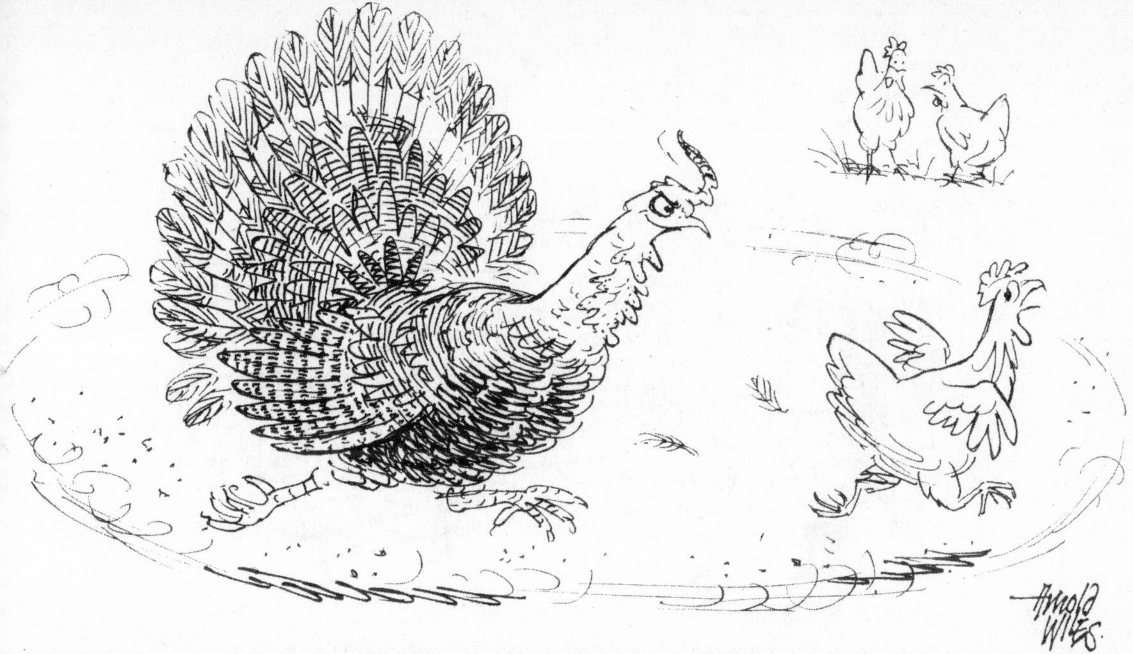
Arnold Wiles

"So much for computer dating."

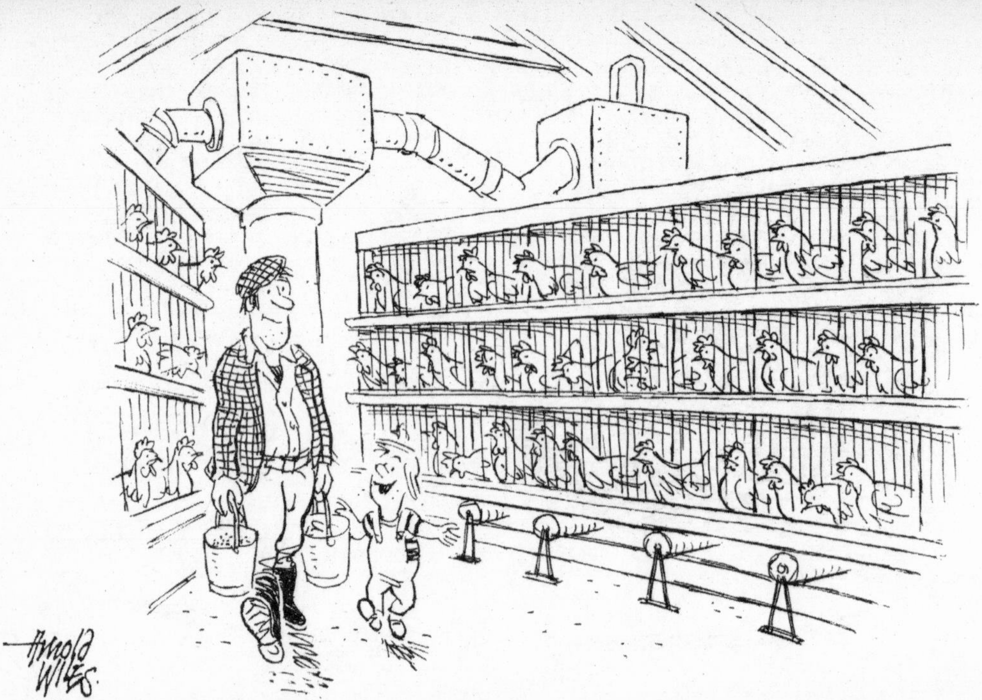

"I expect farming has changed quite a bit since you were incubated."

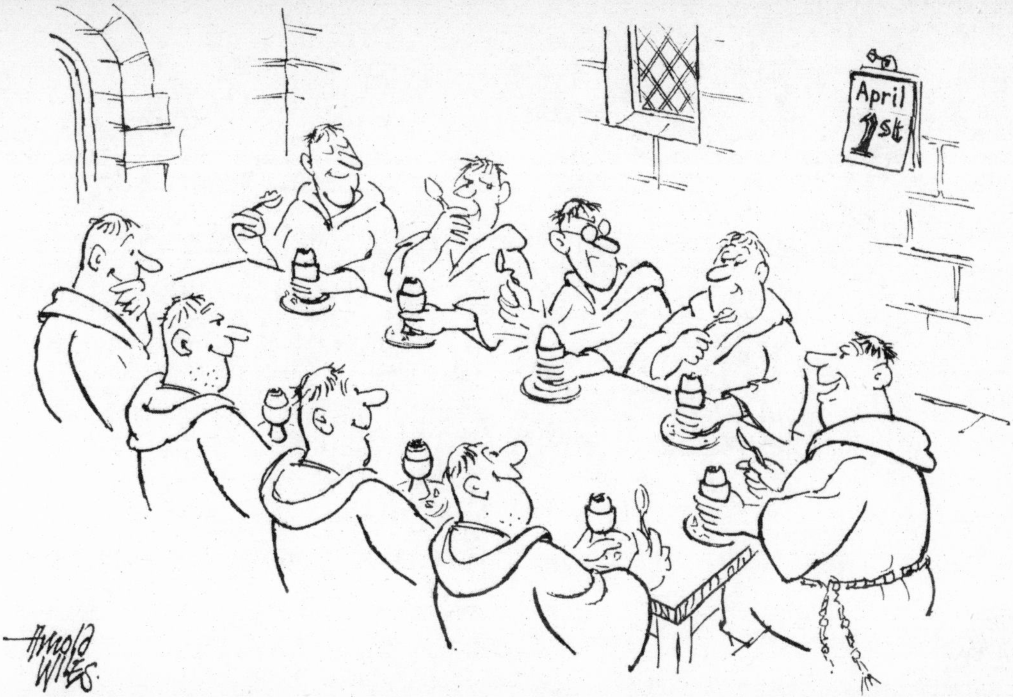
April
1st
Arnold Wiles

"Just our little joke, Brother Andrew. You got the dummy egg."

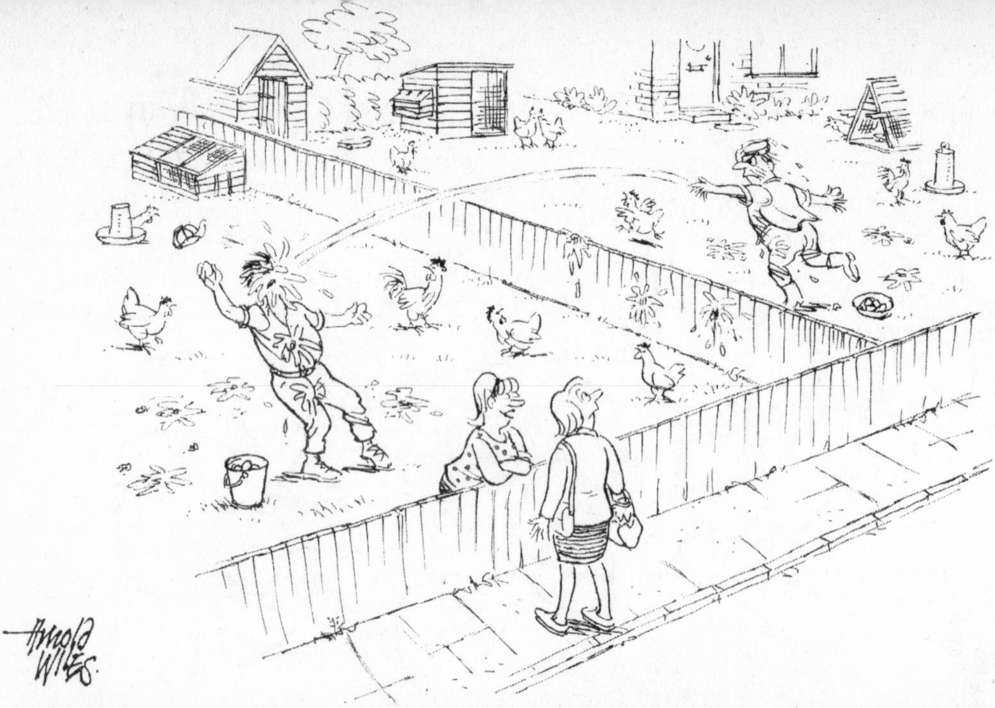

"It all began with a civilised discussion about whose hens were the most prolific layers"

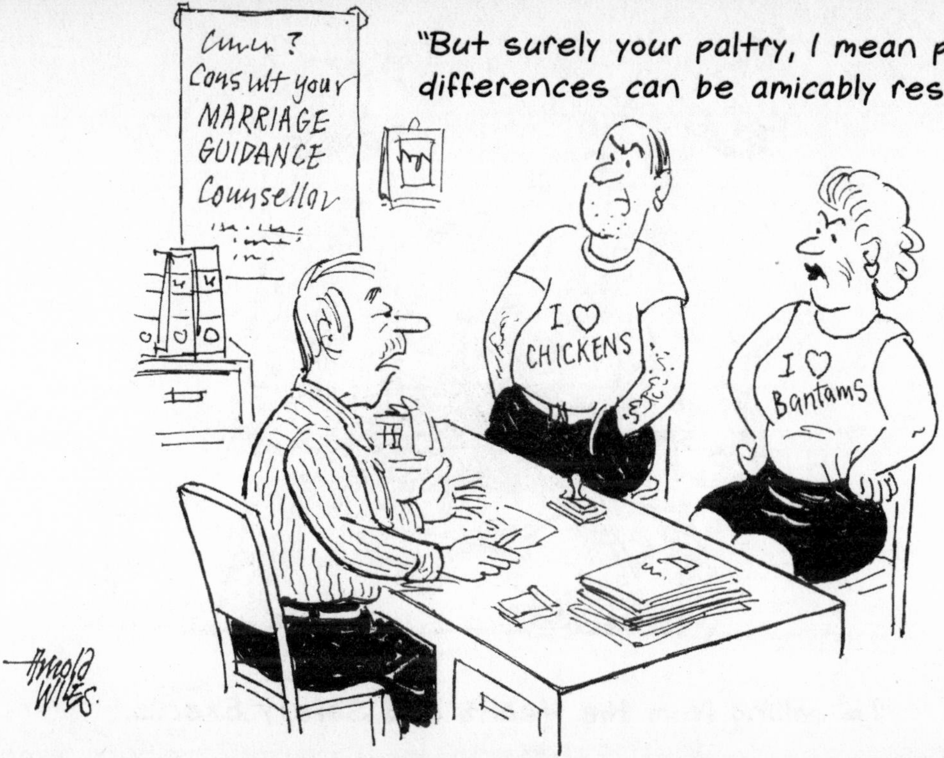
Consult your
MARRIAGE
GUIDANCE
Counsellor
I ♡ CHICKENS
I ♡ Bantams
Arnold Wiles

"But surely your paltry, I mean poultry, differences can be amicably resolved."

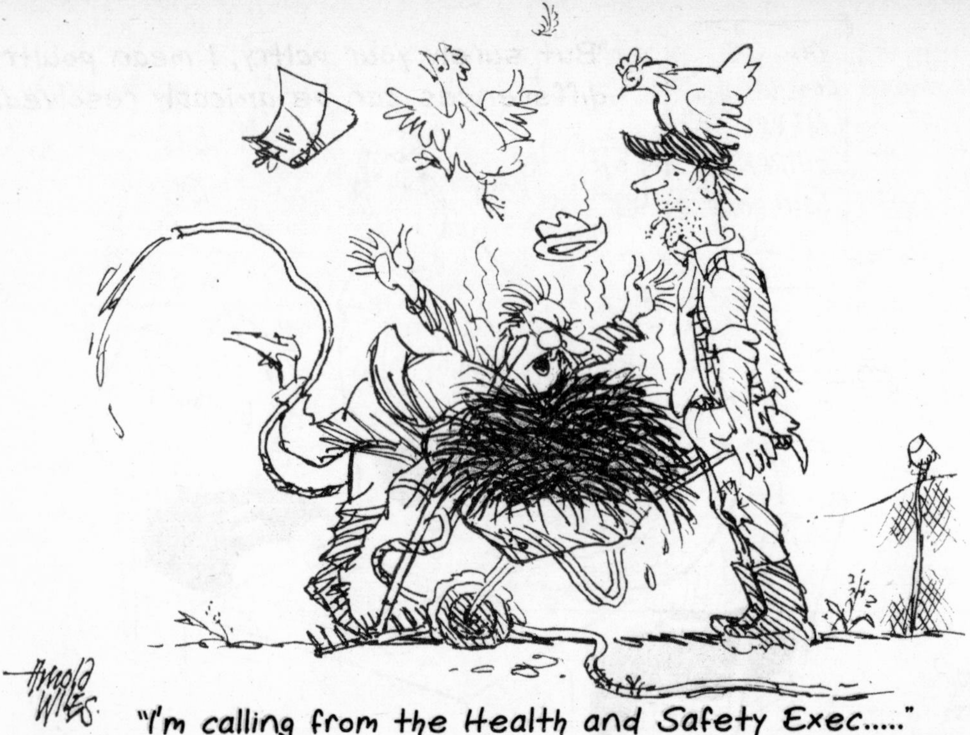

"I'm calling from the Health and Safety Exec....."

"If you don't get a move on, Brother Francis, they'll be well past their 'sell by' date."

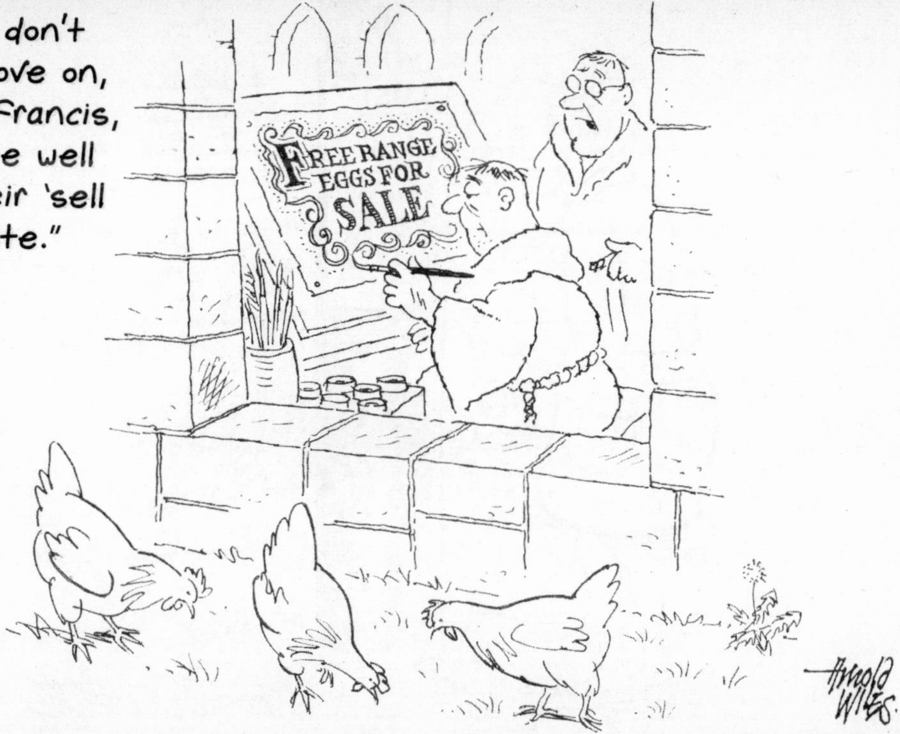
FREE RANGE EGGS FOR SALE
Arnold Wiles

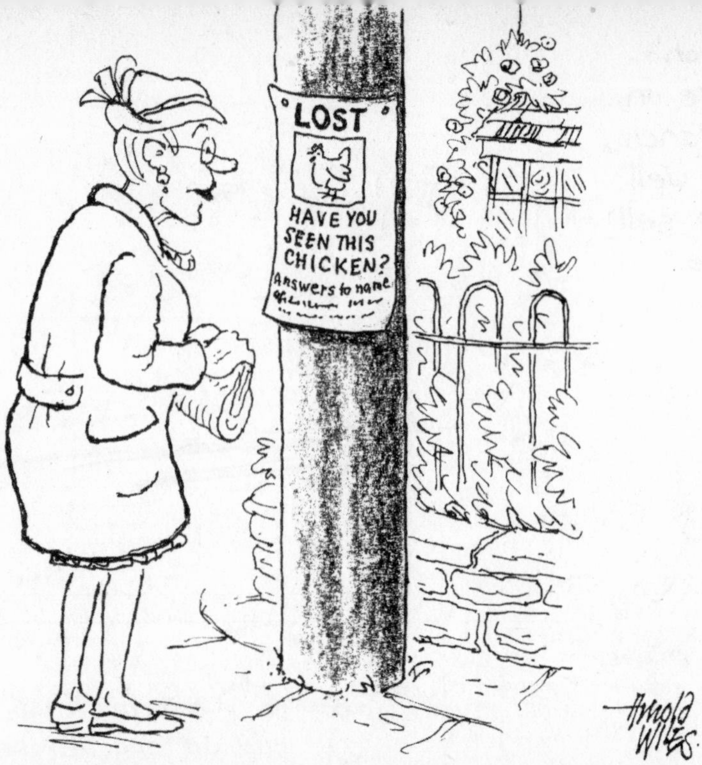
LOST
HAVE YOU SEEN THIS CHICKEN?
Answers to name

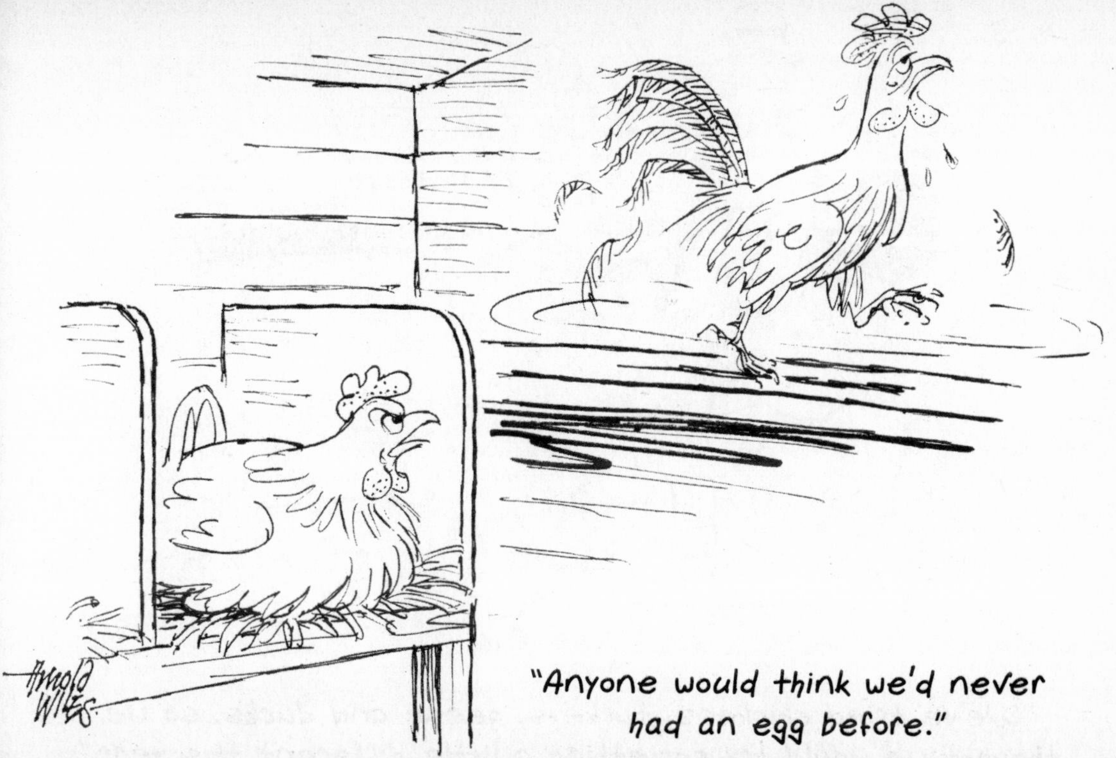
Arnold Wiles

"Anyone would think we'd never had an egg before."

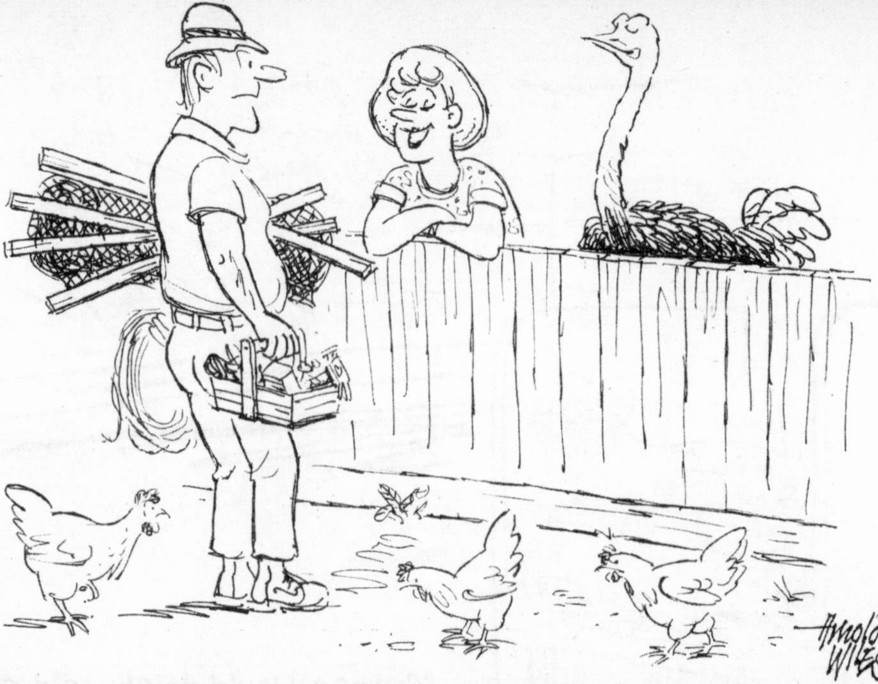
Arnold Wiles

"We've tried chickens, turkeys, geese and ducks, so we thought we would try something a little different this year."

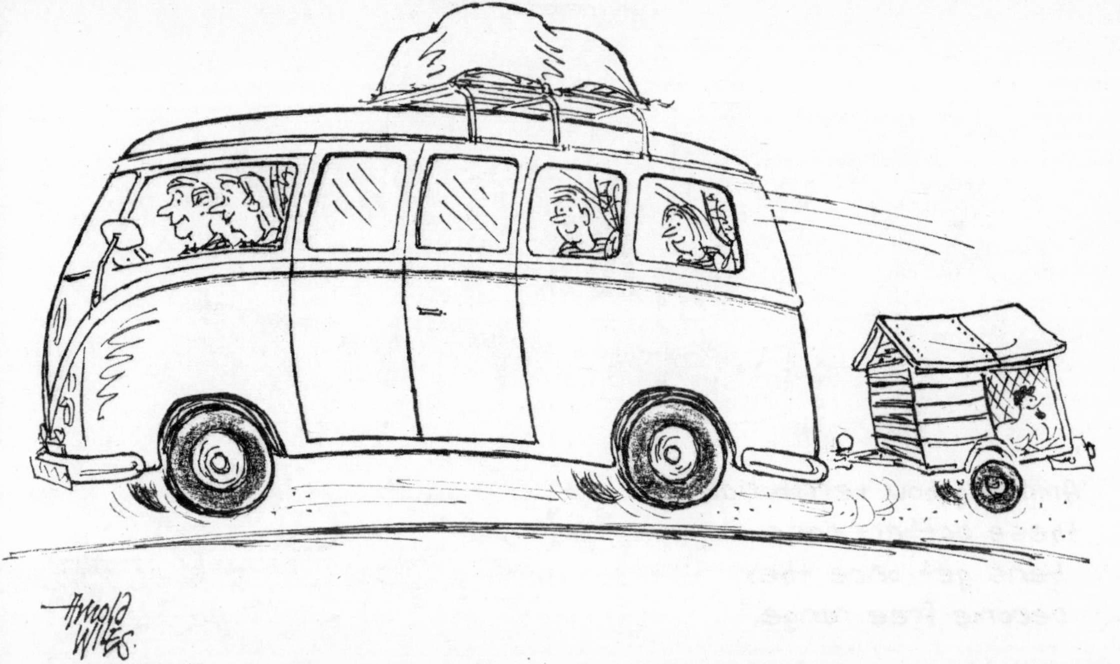
Arnold Wiles

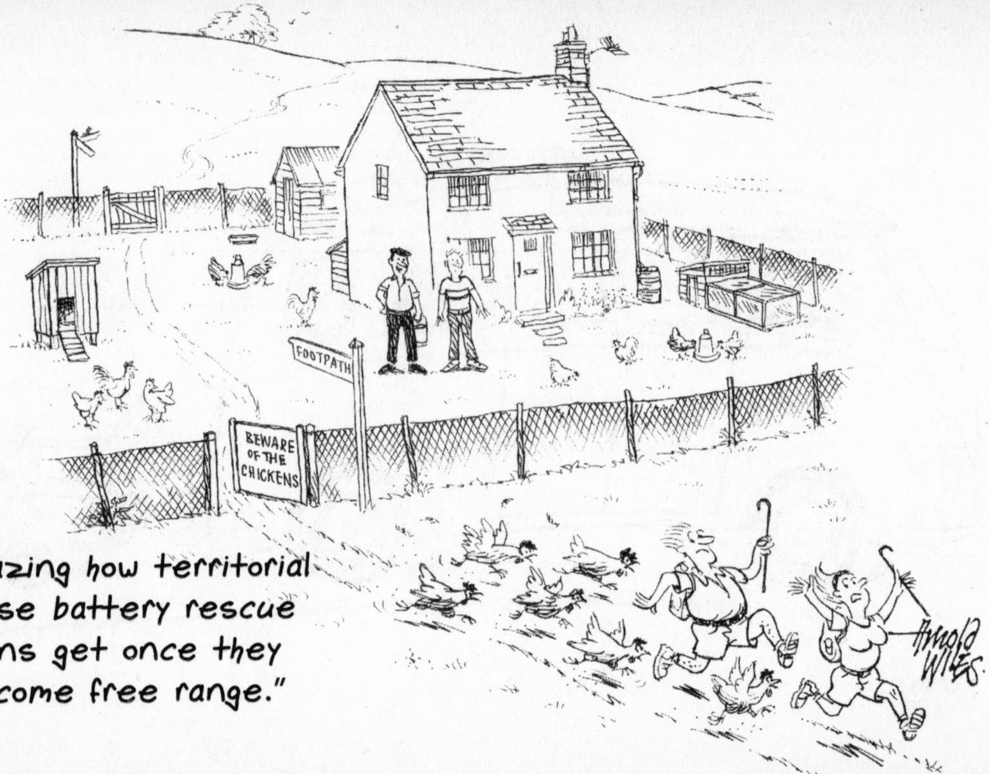
FOOTPATH
BEWARE OF THE CHICKENS
Arnold Wiles

"Amazing how territorial these battery rescue hens get once they become free range."

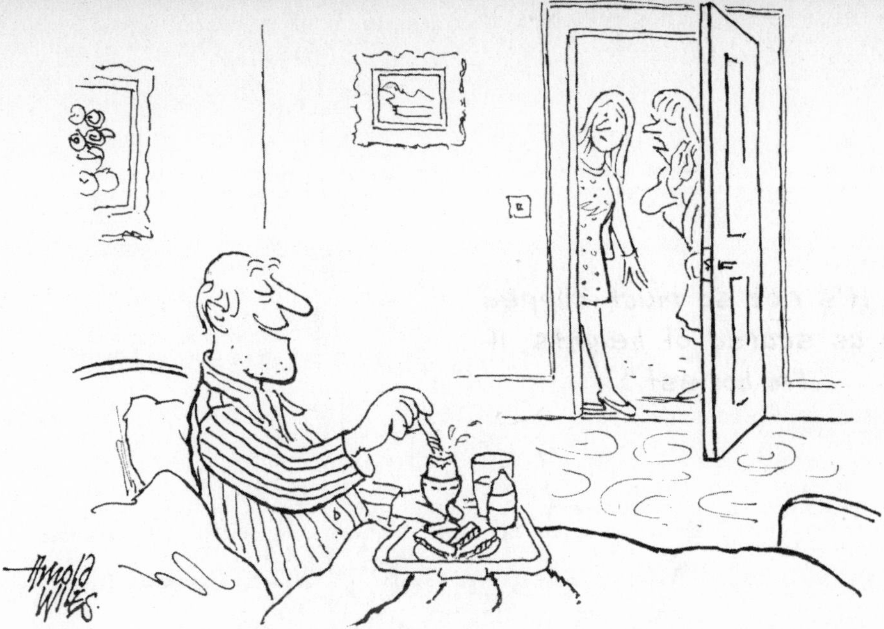
Arnold Wiles

"He's in his second childhood - won't get up till he's had his egg and soldiers."

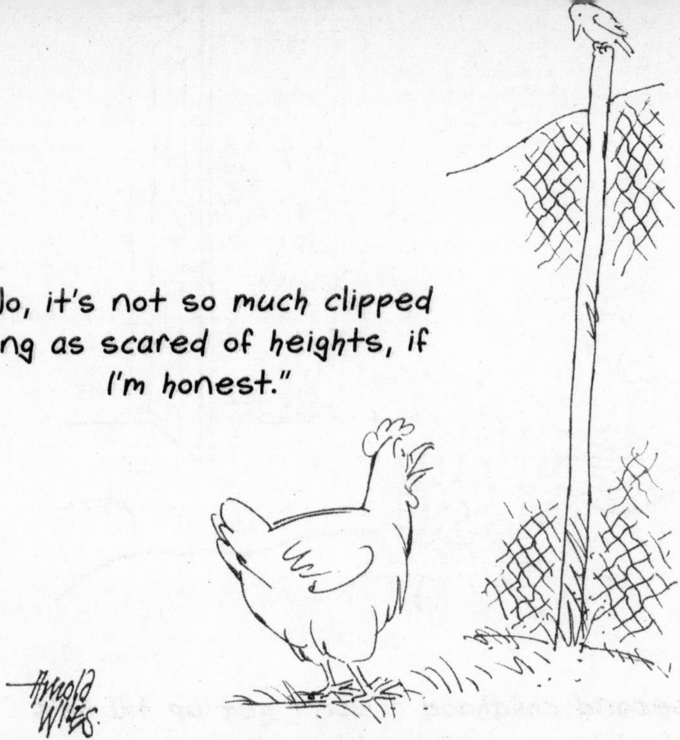
Arnold Wiles

"No, it's not so much clipped wing as scared of heights, if I'm honest."

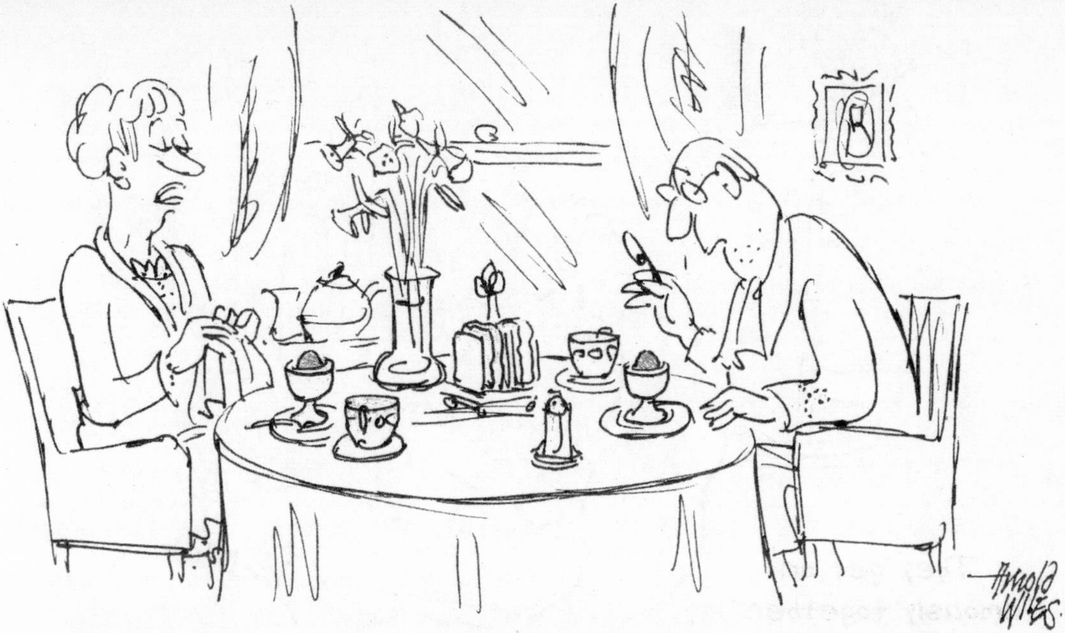
Arnold Wiles

"As it's Lent, I've downsized from large eggs to small."

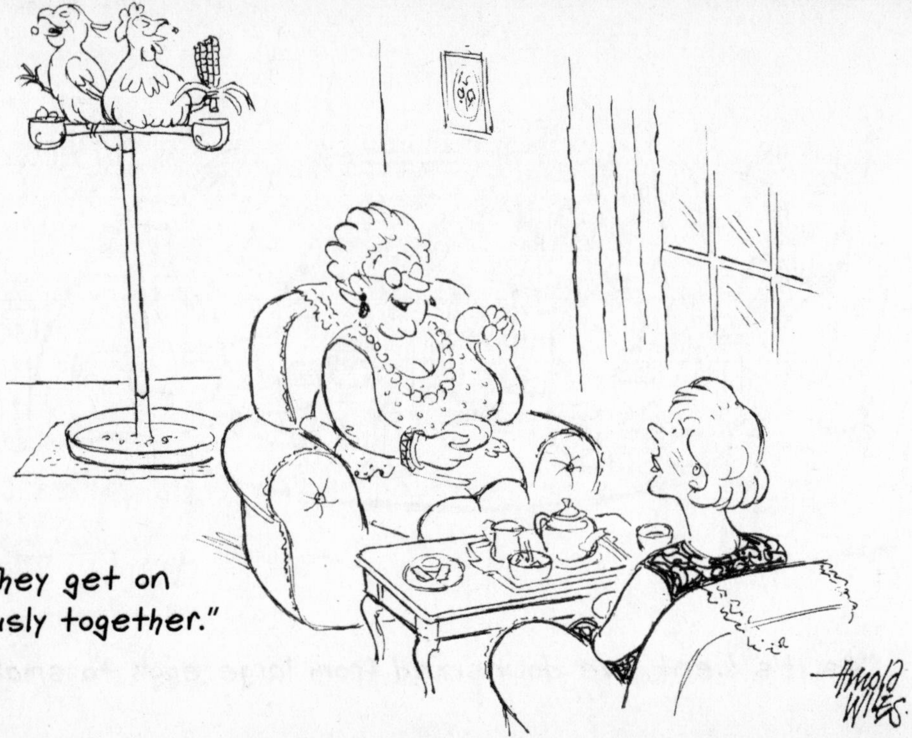
Arnold Wiles

"They get on famously together."

"Now that's what I call enterprising, when the chips are down!"

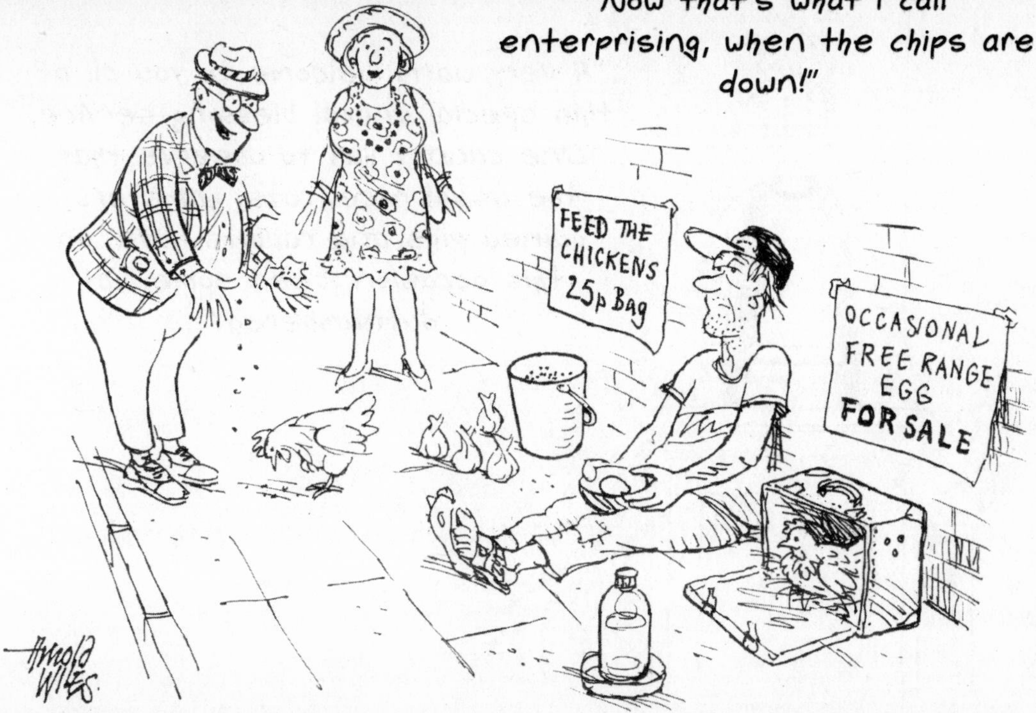
FEED THE CHICKENS 25p Bag
OCCASIONAL FREE RANGE EGG FOR SALE
Arnold Wiles

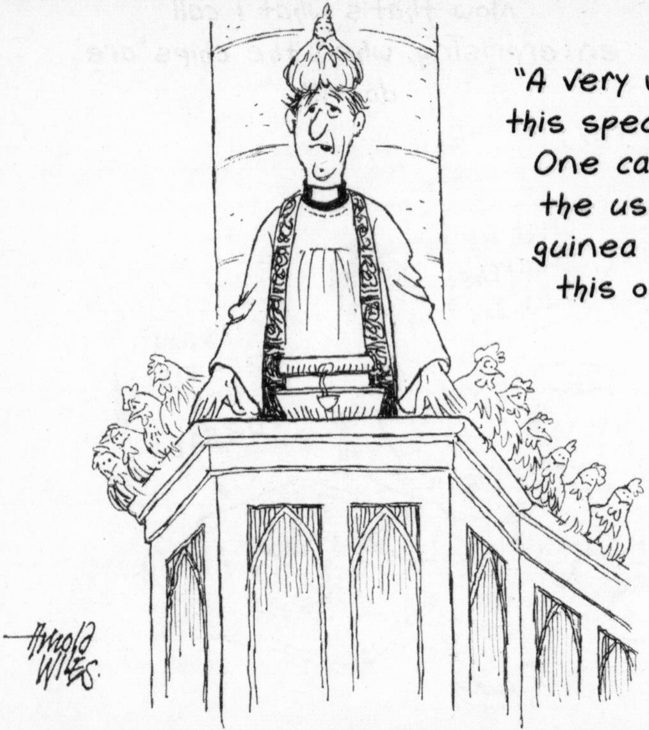

"A very warm welcome to you all at this special animal blessing service. One cannot fail to observe that the usual mice, rats, hamsters, guinea pigs and rabbits have, on this occasion, been somewhat outnumbered."

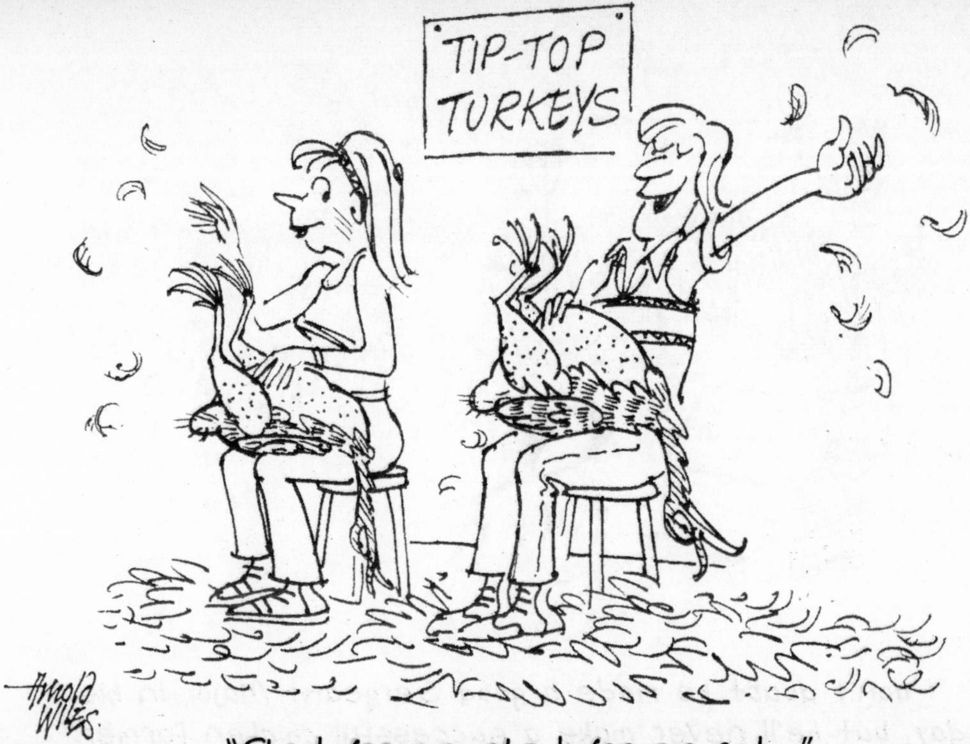
TIP-TOP
TURKEYS
Arnold
Wiles

"She loves me, she loves me not...."

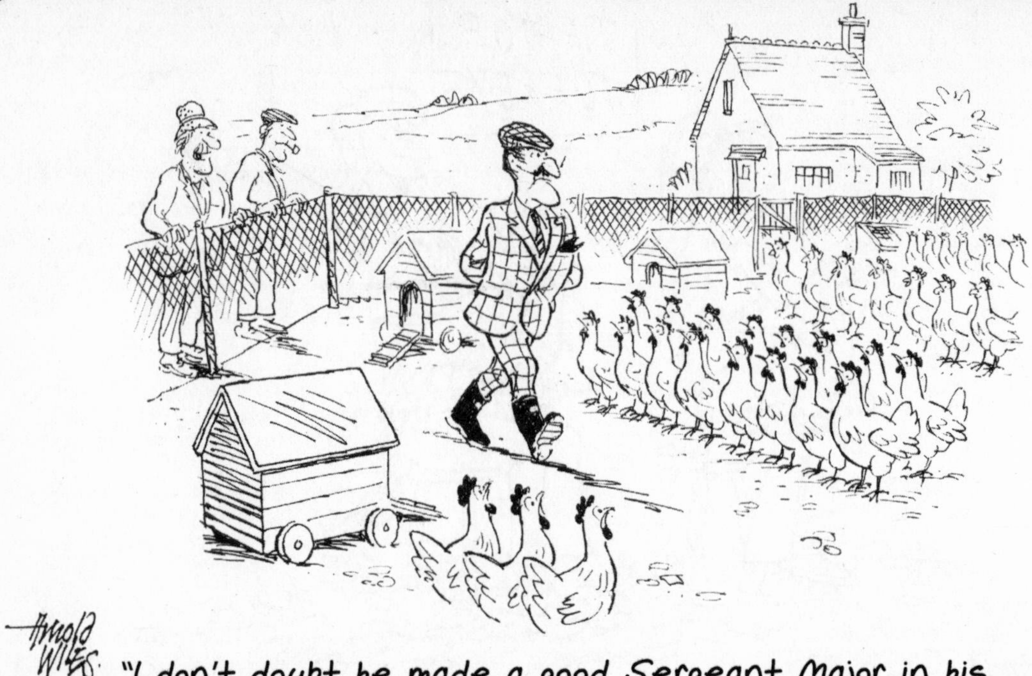
Arnold Wiles

"I don't doubt he made a good Sergeant Major in his day, but he'll never make a successful chicken farmer."

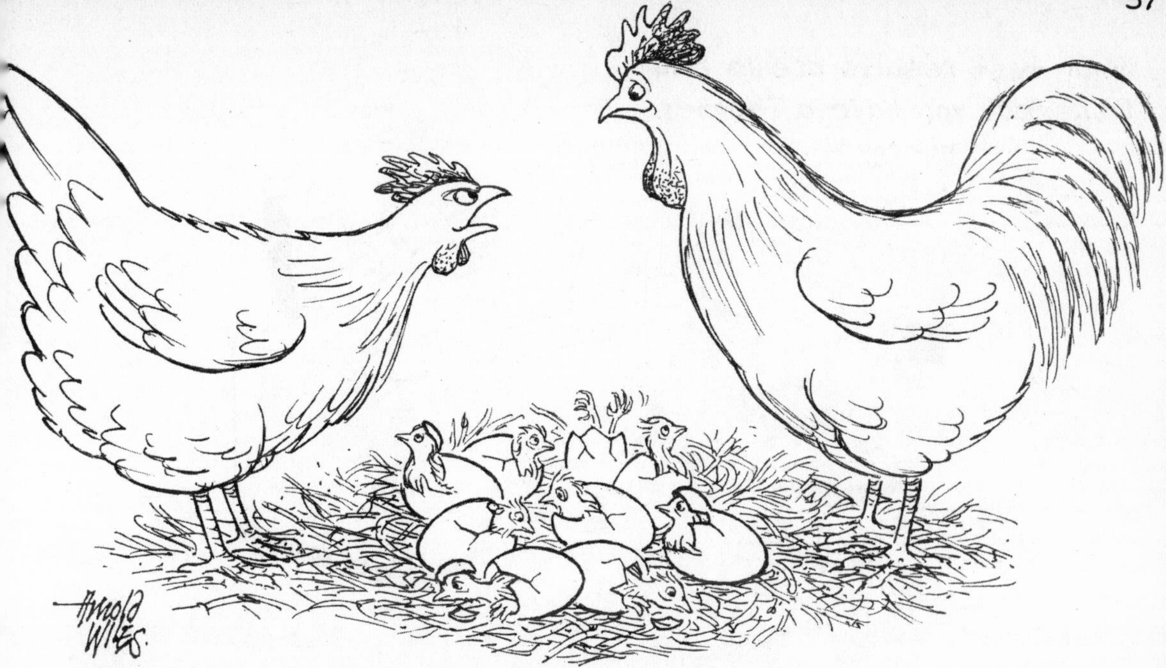

"If you say 'last one out's a sissy' just once more..."

"Your test results are in and I suspect you have a feather allergy."

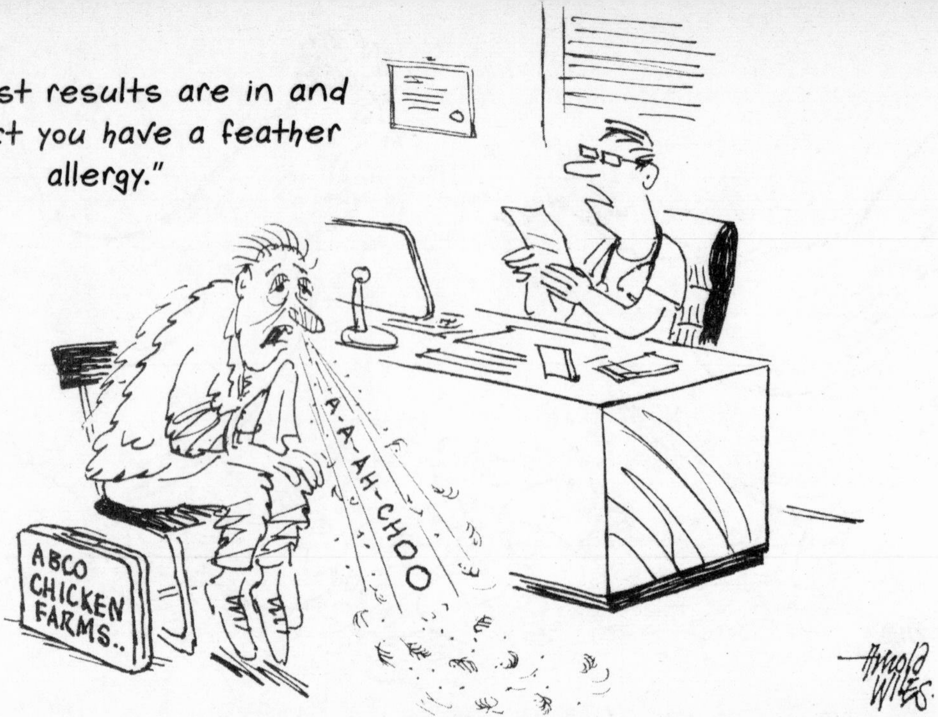
A-A-AH-CHOO
ABCO CHICKEN FARMS..
Arnold Wiles

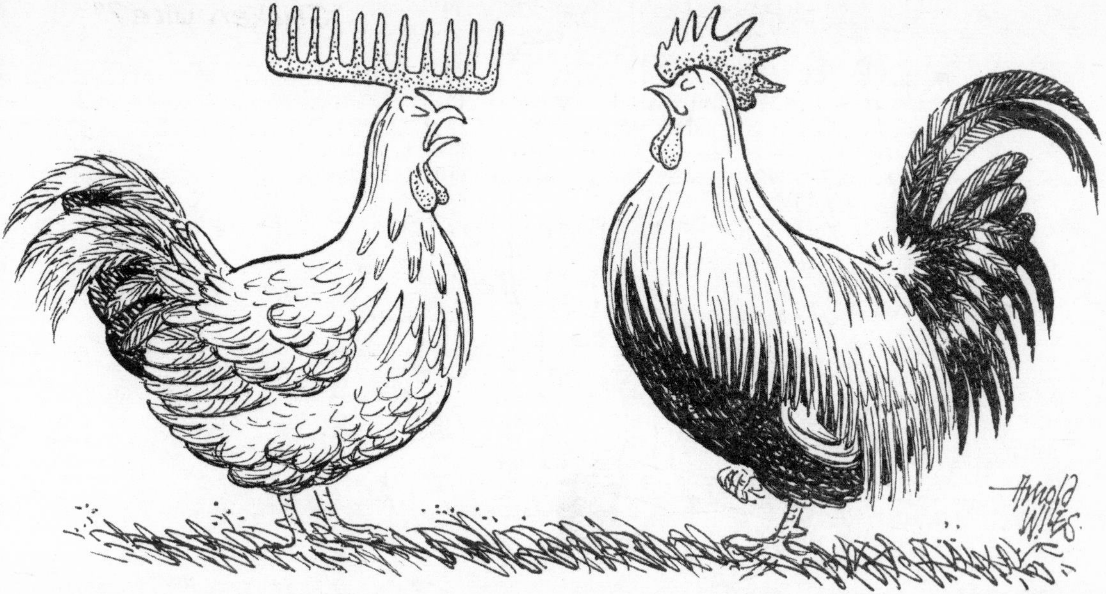

"Don't pretend you've not noticed my beautiful comb. I'll have you know I've been selectively bred for it."

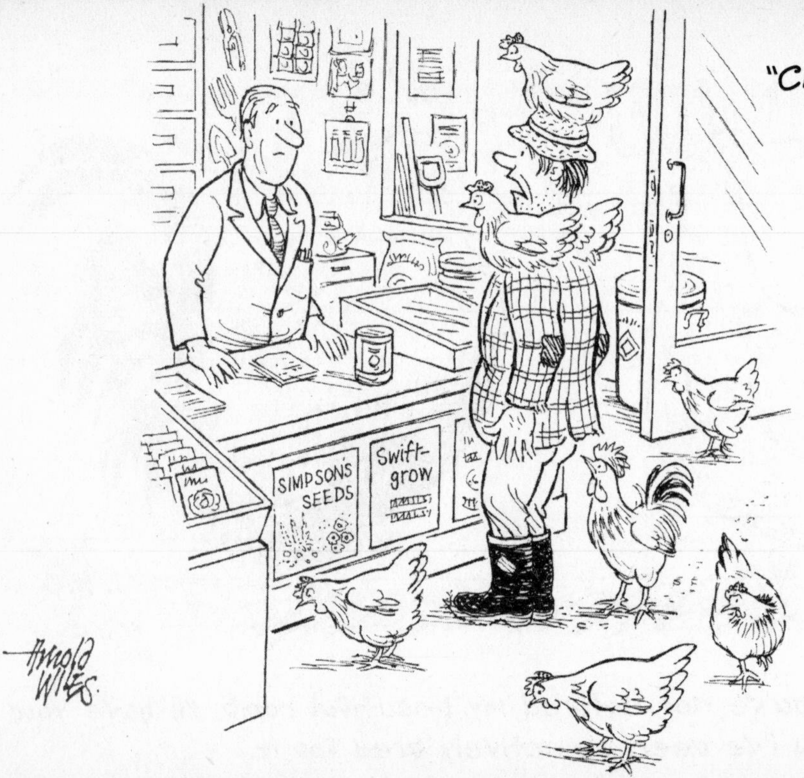
SIMPSON'S SEEDS
Swift-grow
Arnold Wiles

"Chicken wire?"

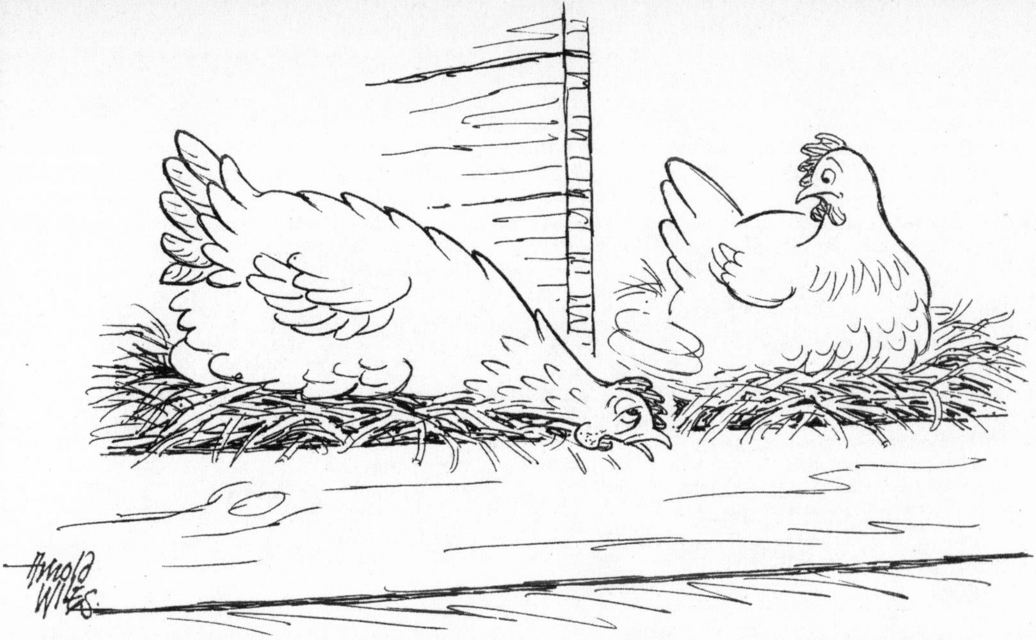
Arnold Wiles

"I could do with a few days off, but I have this damned reputation for laying lots of eggs to live up to."

"I could do with a few days off, but I quite like dashing
backwards and forwards for laying into a cosy nest to live up to."

Both Arnold Wiles and the publishers would like to stress that no chickens were harmed in the making of this book.

The Good Life Press Ltd.
The Old Pigsties
Clifton Fields
Lytham Road
Preston PR4 0XG

The Good Life Press Ltd. publishes a wide range of titles for the smallholder, 'good-lifer' and farmer. We also publish **Home Farmer,** the monthly magazine for anyone who wants to grab a slice of the good life - whether they live in the country or the city. For a complete catalogue please write to the address above, ring us on 01772 633444 or visit our website.

www.goodlifepress.co.uk
www.homefarmer.co.uk